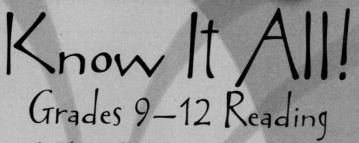

Know It All!
Grades 9–12 Reading
by The Staff of The Princeton Review

Joker

Random House, Inc.
New York

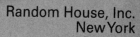

www.randomhouse.com/princetonreview

This workbook was written by The Princeton Review, one of the nation's leaders in test preparation. The Princeton Review helps millions of students every year prepare for standardized assessments of all kinds. The Princeton Review offers the best way to help students excel on standardized tests.

The Princeton Review is not affiliated with Princeton University or Educational Testing Service.

Princeton Review Publishing, L.L.C.
160 Varick Street, 12th Floor
New York, NY 10013

E-mail: textbook@review.com

Published in the United States by Random House, Inc., New York.

ISBN 0-375-76374-0

Editor: Michael Bagnulo
Development Editor: Sherine Gilmour
Production Editor: Diahl Ballard
Director of Production: Iam Williams
Design Director: Tina McMaster
Art Director: Neil McMahon
Production Manager: Mike Rockwitz
Production Coordinator: Greta Blau

Manufactured in the United States of America

9 8 7 6 5 4 3 2 1

First Edition

Contents

Introduction for Parents and Teachers

About This Book

Know It All! focuses on the reading skills that students need to succeed in school and on standardized achievement tests while providing accurate information about an array of fascinating subjects.

Know It All! contains chapters covering important reading skills, regular reviews called Brain Boosters, a practice test, and answers. Each **chapter** focuses on a skill or set of related skills, such as the chapter about vocabulary in context or the chapter about main idea, summary, and theme. The **practice test** was created to resemble the style, structure, difficulty level, and skills common in actual standardized achievement tests. The **answers** offer explanations to the questions on the practice test.

Each **chapter** contains the following:

- an introduction that presents and defines the chapter's skill(s)

- step-by-step explanations of how to apply the chapter's skill(s)

- skill-focused practice passages, multiple-choice, and open-ended questions

There will also be cumulative "Brain Boosters" every four or five chapters to review new skills. Tips throughout the lesson will help students in further developing their skills.

The **practice test** contains the following:

- passages similar in length and difficulty level to passages on actual standardized achievement tests

- multiple-choice and open-ended questions similar in wording and difficulty to questions on actual standardized achievement tests

- a bubble sheet similar to bubble sheets on actual standardized achievement tests for students to fill in their answers to multiple-choice questions

Explanations following the practice test illustrate the best methods to solve each question.

About The Princeton Review

The Princeton Review is one of the nation's leaders in test preparation. We prepare more than two million students every year with our courses, books, online services, and software programs. We help students around the country on many statewide and national standardized tests in a variety of subjects and grade levels. Additionally, we help students on college entrance exams like the SAT-I, SAT-II, and ACT. Our proven strategies and techniques reinforce the skills students learn in the classroom and help them apply these skills to standardized tests.

About Standardized Achievement Tests

Across the nation, different standardized achievement tests are being used to assess students. States choose what tests they want to administer and, often, districts within the state also choose to administer additional tests. Some states administer state-specific tests, which are tests given only in that state and linked to that state's curriculum. Examples of state-specific tests are the Florida Comprehensive Assessment Test (FCAT) or the Massachusetts Comprehensive Assessment System (MCAS). Other states administer national tests, which are tests used in several states in the nation. Examples of some national tests are the Stanford Achievement Test (SAT9), Iowa Test of Basic Skills (ITBS), and TerraNova/CTBS (Comprehensive Test of Basic Skills). Some states administer both state-specific tests and national tests.

Go to http://www.nclb.gov/next/where/statecontacts.html to find out more information about state-specific tests. You can also click on "Assessment Advisor" from the Web site http://k12.princetonreview.com.

Most tests administered to students contain multiple-choice and open-ended questions. Some tests are timed; others are not. Some tests are used to determine if a student can be promoted to the next grade; others are not.

To find out about what test(s) your student will take, when the test(s) will be given, if the test is timed, if it affects grade promotion, or other questions, contact your school or your local school district.

None of the tests can assess all of the unique qualities of your student. They are intended to show how well a student can apply skills they have learned in school in a testing situation.

Because they are connected to a state curriculum, state-specific tests show how well a student can apply the curriculum that was taught in his or her school in a testing situation.

National tests are not connected to a specific state's curricula but have been created to include content that most likely would be taught in your student's grade and subject. Therefore, a national test may be administered to your student to test content that has not been taught in your student's grade or school. National tests show how well a student has done on the test in comparison to other students in the nation have taken that same test.

Student
Introduction

About This Book

What kind of person is a know it all? A know it all craves information and wants to learn new things. A know it all wants to be amazed by what they learn. A know it all is excited by the strange and unusual.

Know It All! is an adventure for your mind. *Know It All!* is full of weird, fascinating, unbelievable articles—all of which contain true information!

In addition to feeding your brain all sorts of interesting information, *Know It All!* will feed your brain with test-taking tips and standardized test practice.

Know It All! contains **chapters, brain boosters,** and a **practice test.**

Each **chapter**

- defines a skill or group of skills such as the chapter about vocabulary in context or the chapter about main idea, summary, and theme
- shows how to use this skill or group of skills to answer an example question
- provides you with practice passages and questions that you may see on standardized tests in school

Each **brain booster**

- reviews the previous few skills
- includes interesting passages to read

The **practice test**

- provides you with passages similar in length and difficulty level to passages on standardized tests
- gives questions similar in wording and difficulty level to questions on standardized tests
- provides a bubble sheet that is similar the type you'll get on standardized achievement tests

You will also receive answers to the questions in the chapters and brain boosters. Also, you will get answers and explanations to the questions in the practice test.

About Standardized Achievement Tests

Standardized Achievement Tests. Who? What? Where? When? Why? How?

You know about them. You've probably taken them. But you might have a few questions about them. If you want to be a *know it all*, then it would be good for you to know about standardized achievement tests.

The words *standardized* and *achievement* describe the word *tests. Standardized* means to compare something with a standard. Standardized tests often use standards that have been decided by your school, district, or state. These standards list the skills you will learn in different subjects in different grades. *Achievement* means the quality of the work produced by a student. So *standardized achievement tests* are tests that assess the quality of your work with certain skills.

To find out the nitty-gritty about any standardized achievement tests you may take, ask your teachers and/or parents. The following are some questions you might want to ask.

Who?   You!

What?   What kinds of questions will be on the test?

               What kinds of skills will be tested by the test?

Where?   Where will the test happen?

When?   When will the test happen?

               How much time will I have to complete the test?

Why?   What affect will my score have?

How?   How should I be prepared?

               Do I need to bring anything to the test?

               If I don't know the answer to a question, should I guess?

None of the tests can assess your unique qualities as a student. They are intended to show how well you can use the skills that you learned in school in a testing situation.

About the Icons in This Book

This book contains many different small pictures called icons. The *icons* tell you about the topics of the passages in this book.

Alternative Animals: Read these passages to learn about animals that you never knew existed and feats that you never knew animals could accomplish. You'll learn about the biggest, smallest, oldest, fastest, and most interesting animals on the planet. You can find these passages in chapters 4, 8, 10, and 15.

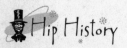

Hip History: Your mission is to storm some of the coolest castles in history with some extraordinary historical figures—some of whom aren't much older than you. These passages will help you complete that mission, while learning the most interesting stories in history. You can find these passages in chapters 4, 6, 7, 9, and 12.

For Your Amusement: You want to play games? Read these passages to learn about cool games, toys, amusement parks, and festivals. You can find these passages in chapters 5, 7, 8, and 11.

Extreme Sports: Read these passages to learn about outrageous contests, wacky personalities, and incredible feats in the world of sports. You can find these passages in chapters 1, 2, 5, and 6.

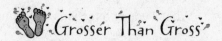

Grosser Than Gross: How gross can you get? Read these passages if you want to learn about really gross things. Be warned: Some of the passages may be so gross that they're downright scary. You can find these passages in chapters 1, 3, 6, and 11.

Mad Science: If you read these passages, you'll see science like you've never seen it before. You'll learn about all sorts of interesting science-related stuff. You can find these passages in chapters 2, 3, 11, and 12.

 **Outer Space Oddities**

Outer-Space Oddities: Do you ever wonder what goes on in the universe away from planet Earth? Satisfy your curiosity by reading a passage about astronomical outer-space oddities. You can find this passage in chapter 13.

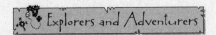 Explorers and Adventurers

Explorers and Adventurers: Did you ever want to take a journey to learn more about a place? Well, you'll get the opportunity to do that when you read a passage about explorers and adventurers. You can find this passage in chapter 8.

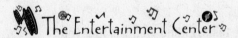 The Entertainment Center

The Entertainment Center: Do you enjoy listening to music or watching television and movies? Well, here's your chance to read about them! You can find these passages in chapters 3, 4, 9, 10, and 13.

 Art-rageous

Art-rageous: Are you feeling a bit creative? Read these passages to get an unusual look into art that's all around you: books, drawings, paintings, and much more. You can find these passages in chapters 5, 14, and 16.

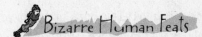 Bizarre Human Feats

Bizarre Human Feats: People do some very strange stuff. You can read about some of these incredible-but-true human feats things. You can find this passage in chapter 16.

 WILD CARDS

Wild Cards: You'll never know what you're going to get with these passages. It's a mixed bag. Anything goes! You can find these passages in chapters 7, 9, 10, 12, 13, 14, 15, and 16.

Things to Remember When Preparing for Tests

There are lots of things you can do to prepare for standardized achievement tests. Here are a few examples.

- **Work hard in school all year.** Working hard in school all year is a great way to prepare for tests.

- **Read.** Read everything you can. Read your homework, your textbooks, the newspaper, magazines, novels, plays, poems, comics, even the back of the cereal box. Reading a lot is a great way to prepare for tests.

- **Work on this book!** This book provides you with loads of practice for tests. You've probably heard the phrase, "Practice makes perfect." Practice can be a great way to prepare for tests.

- **Ask your teachers and/or parents questions about your schoolwork whenever you don't understand something.** Your teachers and your parents can help you with your schoolwork. Asking for help when you need it is a great way to prepare for tests and to become a *know it all*.

- **Ask your teachers and/or parents for information about the tests.** If you have questions about the tests, ask them! Being informed is a great way to prepare for tests.

- **Have a good dinner and a good breakfast before the tests.** Eating well will fuel your body with energy, and your brain thrives on energy. You want to take the test with all the engines ready in your brain.

- **Get enough sleep before the tests.** Being awake and alert while taking tests is very important. Your body and your mind work best when you've had enough sleep. So get some Zs on the nights before the tests!

- **Check your work.** When taking a test, you may end up with extra time. You could spend that extra time twiddling your toes or timing how long you can go without blinking. But if you use extra time to check your work, you might spot some mistakes—and improve your score.

- **Stay focused.** You may find that your mind has wandered away from the test once in a while. Don't worry—it happens. Just say to your brain, "Brain, it's great that you are so curious, imaginative, and energetic. But I need to focus on the test now." Your brain will thank you later.

The Chapters

CHAPTER 1
Multiple-Choice and Open-Response Questions

What made a professional skateboarder want to create skateboard parks throughout the United States?

How do we express feelings when we are writing e-mails?

What happened to a boat filled with tons of garbage that no one wanted?

On your way to becoming a *know it all*, you will need to know how to answer multiple-choice and open-response questions.

Chances are by now you have encountered **multiple-choice questions** on tests. These questions ask you for information and then provide you with some answer choices. The great thing about multiple-choice questions is that the best answer is always right there before your eyes! In this book, multiple-choice questions will follow passages that are about cool and unusual things. You will want to read those passages carefully before answering the multiple-choice questions.

After you read the passage on the next page, you will learn all about the **Know It All Approach** to answering multiple-choice questions. You will be able to use this approach throughout this book, and on standardized achievement tests too.

Open-response questions ask you to write something about what you have read using information found in the reading passage. An open-response question may ask you to compare two characters or ideas, or to describe something that you have read about. While you need to refer to the passage to answer the question, open-response questions allow you to be a little bit creative in your approach to showing what you know. In this book, open-response questions will follow passages that are about cool and unusual things. You will want to read those passages carefully before answering the open-response questions.

After you read the passage on the next page, you will learn all about the **Know It All Approach** to answering open-response questions. You will be able to use this approach throughout this book, and on standardized achievement tests too.

Ready to begin your journey to *know it all*? Begin your journey to *knowing it all* by getting on board with the example passage on the next page.

 Extreme Sports

In Search of a Place to Skate

Would you believe that almost eleven million Americans own and ride skateboards? Furthermore, it's estimated that more than a million people are newcomers to the sport every year. Despite its popularity, there aren't too many places where people can legally skate. In fact, there are only about 700 skate parks nationwide. Only about half of these parks are open to the public. Many skateboarders must find or build their own spaces in which to practice free from traffic and pedestrians. Unfortunately, these skaters are often yelled at, ticketed, or even arrested for skating in "forbidden places." Imagine calling home from jail to say, "I've been arrested for skateboarding!"

Luckily for skaters, communities are beginning to recognize the need to build more places for skaters to safely ride. Tony Hawk, the legendary former pro-skateboard superstar, has played a powerful role in the skate-park movement. Tony Hawk established the non-profit Tony Hawk Foundation to help promote, fund, and build skate parks in the United States. His love for skating began when he was nine years old, so he understands that skaters should be encouraged develop their skills and not be criticized as "lawbreakers."

The building of skate parks is new to many cities. Public officials often have to be persuaded to hire designers and builders who are experienced with the kind of construction that is unique to skating ramps and jumps. Once the new skate parks are finished, they often become the most popular recreational facilities in town. Tony Hawk's mission to create parks to keep skateboarders safe is his best feat yet!

▶ According to the passage, what did Tony Hawk establish to help skateboarders?

A   new moves for skateboarding
B   about 700 skate parks nationwide
C   the most popular and fastest-growing sport
D   the Tony Hawk Foundation

▶ Describe how Tony Hawk probably feels about skateboarding. Support your answer with details from the passage.

_____

_____

Now that you have gone for a ride, stop and look at the sample questions.

Steps for Answering Multiple-Choice Questions

The **Know It All Approach** to answering multiple-choice questions consists of eight steps. Read on to learn all about them. As you go through each step, consider the multiple-choice question following "In Search of a Place to Skate."

Step 1

Read the passage carefully.

In this book and on most standardized achievement tests, you will be asked multiple-choice questions about passages that you have read. While reading passages, feel free to underline or highlight words and take notes in the margins.

Step 2

Read the question carefully.

This will help you to determine exactly what the question is asking. Look at the multiple-choice question following the passage you just read: *According to the passage, what did Tony Hawk establish to help skateboarders?*

You will want to take special note of words such as *not* or *except*. Usually, these words ask you to find the answer choice that contradicts information given in the passage or is the exception among the answer choices. Words such as *effect* and *because* in a question indicate that the question is asking about a cause-and-effect relationship. The words *according to* indicate that the question is asking for the answer that is correct from a particular point of view.

Step 3

Think of the answer in your own words.

In your own words, what do you think may be the answer to the question: *According to the passage, what did Tony Hawk establish to help skateboarders?*

Step 4 · Read all of the answer choices.

Look for the answer choice that is the most similar to the answer you came up with on your own and that best answers the question. Even if you think you have found the correct answer after reading the first answer choice, read ALL of the answer choices to make sure there is none that are better answers.

Go through all of the answer choices in the sample question. What do you think about answer choice (A)? While Tony Hawk may have invented new moves for skateboarding, is that information included in the passage? Look back and check. You may know that Tony Hawk did create new skateboarding moves, but the passage does not mention that information. Answer choice (A) is not correct.

What about answer choice (B)? While "about 700 skate parks nationwide" is mentioned in the passage, is Tony Hawk credited with establishing those parks? The passage does not state that Tony Hawk established those parks; rather, it claims that there are "only about 700 skate parks nationwide." Dump answer choice (B).

What about answer choice (C)? Does the passage claim that Tony Hawk established skateboarding? Although, the passage claims that skateboarding is one of the most popular and fastest-growing sports, it does not state that Tony Hawk invented it. Answer choice (C) is wrong.

What about answer choice (D)? In the second paragraph, you have read that Tony Hawk established the Tony Hawk Foundation to promote and provide funds for high-quality public skateboard parks throughout the United States. Therefore, answer choice (D) is correct.

Step 5 · Double-check your answer.

You can double-check your answer by referring again to the passage or rereading the question.

To double-check this answer, reread the question and look back at the passage. While you may have known information about Tony Hawk and skateboarding, the correct answer was supported by information in the passage. Always use information in the passage to identify the correct answer.

Step 6 · For questions that you are unable to answer, use Process of Elimination.

Process of Elimination can help you to find the correct answer to a difficult multiple-choice question. Even if you have not been able to identify answer, you may be able to identify *incorrect answer choices*. Do any of the answer choices contradict information provided in the reading selection? If so, you can ditch that answer.

You may be able to eliminate three answer choices, leaving you with only one answer choice. If that happens, choose the remaining answer choice because there is a good chance that it is the correct answer. You may only be able to eliminate one or two answer choices. If so, guess from the remaining answer choices. By eliminating even one answer choice, you have increased your chances of picking the correct answer.

While you did not have to use Process of Elimination this time, you can see how going through each answer choice and crossing out choices (A), (B), and (C) would have led you to the correct answer, (D).

Steps for Answering Open-Response Questions

The **Know It All Approach** to answering open-response questions consists of six steps. Read on to learn all about them. As you go through each step, consider the open-response question following "In Search of a Place to Skate."

Step 1   **Read the passage carefully.**

In this book and on most standardized achievement tests, you will be asked open-response questions about passages that you have read.

Step 2   **Read the question carefully.**

By reading carefully, you should be able to determine exactly what the question is asking.

Look at the open-response question following the passage you just read: *Describe how Tony Hawk probably feels about skateboarding. Support your answer with details from the passage.*

Step 3   **Read the question again and underline the words that tell you what you need to do in order to write the best possible answer.**

Take special notice of words that tell you what to do. Some of these words are *explain, describe, compare,* and *contrast.* Notice any words in the question that will help you in forming your response? How about the word *describe*? This tells you that you will need to explain how Tony Hawk probably feels about skateboarding.

Step 4

Plan your answer.

As you think about writing your answer, be sure to return to the passage and check the words you underlined or the notes you wrote. Also, be sure to use only the information provided in the passage in your answer.

What information can you use from the passage to support your answer? The passage does state the following: "His love for skating began when he was only nine years old, so he understands that skaters should be encouraged to develop their skills and not be criticized as 'lawbreakers.'" You can use that information to support your answer.

Step 5

Write your answer neatly and clearly.

Here is a sample answer to the open-response question: *Describe how Tony Hawk probably feels about skateboarding. Support your answer with details from the passage.*

Tony Hawk probably loves skateboarding just as much now as he did when he was nine years old. By starting up the Tony Hawk Foundation, he is helping to create high-quallity public skateboard parks throughout the United States. Tony beleives that kids should not be labeled as outcasts because of their favorite sport.

Step 6

Revise.

After writing your answer, read the question and your answer again. Check that you have fully answered the question, included important information from the passage to support your answer, and checked your answer for any errors in punctuation, spelling, usage, or grammar

Look at the sample answer above. Does it answer the question? It describes how Tony Hawk probably feels about skating by stating he "probably loves skateboarding just as much now as he did when he was nine years old." Does it use details from the passage? It mentions the Tony Hawk Foundation as well as the details about when Tony began skating. Can you find any errors in punctuation, spelling, usage, or grammar? The word *quality* is misspelled, and so is the word *believes*.

You did it! Now that you know how to answer multiple-choice and open-response questions the **Know It All** way, it's time for you to give it a go!

How Does a Word Say Cheese?

Imagine trying to have a conversation with a friend while you are wearing a suit of armor that covers your face and body. You would probably have a hard time letting your friend know if you are happy, sad, annoyed, or excited. That is the problem when you communicate through printed words. Chances are, if you use e-mail, you have contemplated the tone of an e-mail message. What did the sender mean? Is he angry with me? Is she being sarcastic? Because the person you are talking to cannot see you, how do you convey the feelings behind what you are saying? Emoticons, of course! The first emoticon, an electronic version of the smiley face, was invented more than twenty years ago by Scott E. Fahlman, a computer science professor.

Emoticons are facial expressions created by a certain series of symbols on the computer keyboard. These keystroke combinations often produce an image of a face sideways, which helps the reader feel the "tone" of the words instead of just reading them. The language of keyboard-coded expressions includes: smiling faces :-), faces showing wide-eyed shock 8-o, and faces showing winking ;-). The world of emoticons, however, does not stop there. In fact, there are web dictionaries that list vast varieties of emoticons.

1. What did Scott E. Fahlman create more than twenty years ago?

   A   e-mail acronyms
   B   the word *cheese*
   C   the computer smiley face*
   D   e-mail communication

2. Emoticons can do all of the following **except**

   A   let you know a friend is joking.
   B   express wide-eyed shock.
   C   help to give tone to an email.
   D   send e-mails to your friends.*

   :-(= frowning   :-D = ha-ha

   :-o = oh no!   :-* = here's a kiss

   :'-(= crying   =^..^= = cat

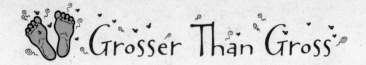
A Load of Garbage

Most likely, you would not want to take in someone else's garbage, especially if it weighed tons and was potentially poisonous!

Loaded with almost 3,200 tons of New York City trash, Mobro 4000, better known as the Mobro Barge, or the garbage barge, began its journey from Long Island to North Carolina in March 1987. The voyage was part of a business plan of moving garbage from the New York City region to southern states. Because many southern states were less populated, the landfill costs were cheaper. En route, North Carolina officials learned that the trash on the barge included hazardous waste from hospitals, like used dressing gowns and syringes. They decided the garbage was toxic. As a result, North Carolina refused to accept the garbage. The Mobro anchored off local shores for eleven days and then was ordered to sail away.

The garbage barge made its way to Louisiana, the home of the Mobro Barge and its captain. Louisiana, which had its own environmental issues, refused to take on New York's smelly problem. The Mobro then headed into the Gulf of Mexico. The Mexican Navy met the garbage barge in the Yucatán Channel and prevented it from entering Mexican waters. Belize would not take the trash, either. Before it headed back to New York, the Mobro Barge was rejected by six states and three countries and had logged 6,000 miles!

The barge's next stop was Queens, New York. That was the plan, until the borough president of Queens obtained a temporary restraining order that forced the Mobro to stay away. As summer approached, the barge sat anchored off the shores of Brooklyn. The debate over what to do with its load was a topic for the courts. In July 1987, the Mobro was granted anchorage in New Jersey by the federal government. In October, an agreement was finally reached! The Mobro's cargo was at last burned to ashes (430 tons of it!) and buried in a landfill on Long Island, New York—from where the barge had first sailed!

3. Explain why you think six states and three countries rejected the garbage barge. Support your answer with details from the passage.

_____

_____

Subject Review

Are you ready to cruise along and use the **Know It All Approach** to answer multiple-choice and open-response questions? Are you smiling about the choices you will encounter? Excited to get past the garbage and respond using the fun and cool facts you will come across? Then get started!

First, some helpful reminders to keep you on track to becoming a *know it all*. Always, read the passages and questions carefully! You don't want to miss out on learning any of this good stuff, do you? When answering multiple-choice and open-response questions use **only** information from the passage to answer questions! For multiple-choice questions be sure to read all of the answer choices before you choose your answer.

Now you should be able to answer the questions from the beginning of the chapter.

What made a professional skateboarder want to create skateboard parks throughout the United States?
The fact that kids are in need of skateboard parks to practice their moves in safe, skateboard-friendly zones.

How do we express feelings when we are writing e-mails?
Emoticons of course! :-)

What happened to a boat filled with tons of garbage that no one wanted?
It headed back to its native New York, where its cargo was reduced to ashes. The remains, 430 tons of ash, were buried at a landfill in Long Island, New York.

CHAPTER 2
Details

What does "mostabc peopleabc shedabc 45670 poundsabc ofabc skinabc inabc aabc lifetimeabc" mean?

What title did Wilma Rudolph earn in 1960?

What three events might have led to the extinction of the dinosaurs?

L earn why every word counts by completing this chapter about details.

Details and Supporting Details

Details are the facts and particulars that make articles, poems, and stories more interesting to read. They tell you specific information about people, events, and places. Why do you need details? Well, imagine that your friend was having a party for you before you went away for the summer. You would want to tell your friend when you were leaving—otherwise your friend might end up throwing your party when you were already gone! So, you would share the detail of your departure date with your friend. You would probably want to share some other details as well, such as who you would like to invite, what kind of music you would like to be played, and what kind of food to eat. (Okay, that's enough—you wouldn't want your friend to think you're pushy or anything, would you?) Details generally answer the questions: who, what, when, where, why, and how.

Supporting details are facts and particulars that support the overall meaning of an article, poem, or story. Authors use supporting details to convey tone, to persuade, and to present information so that the readers can reach their own conclusions. Supporting details function much like a supporting cast does in a movie or television show. Consider your favorite movie or television show. There is usually one main star. So what are all of the other characters doing there? They interact with the main character and to help that character "develop" or become more like a real person. You get to learn more about the main character through the supporting characters. The same holds true for supporting details—they help you to learn more about a topic.

Be a *know it all* by sharing these details and supporting details with friends.

- Let your friends know that birds have many different songs that they can sing. Support this fact, by informing your friends that birds sing different songs in order to communicate about feeding, nesting, flying, and protecting their young.

- Let your friends know that woodpeckers don't get headaches from hammering. Support this fact, by informing your friends that woodpeckers' heads are filled with pockets of air that cushion their head bones as they drill for food or create the tunnels that lead to their nests.

Cracking Codes

You are secret agent KIA, one of the agency's newest recruits. With the help of your trusty codebook, you may be asked to decode important messages that could affect what you know. The future of your knowledge may rest in your ability to crack the code. First, KIA's code maker will let you in on the new code to add to your codebook: *after every word, insert "abc"; after number "4" insert "567"*. Now, try to crack this secret message using the cipher, or code. The code is the system of altering the text to hide its meaning.

Youabc useabc 14567 muclesabc toabc smileabc andabc 45673 toabc frownabc.

Did you complete your first mission as secret agent KIA?

The science of secret communication through codes is called *cryptology*. There is evidence that the use of secret writing, or *cryptography,* dates back to ancient civilizations. Today, cryptography is used by governments, the military, businesses, institutions, and individuals to protect important messages and business transactions. You may already be familiar with codes like Braille, Morse code, pig latin, and computer code.

To solve *cryptograms,* which are quotations, sayings, or texts that have been coded, code breakers study words. They look for patterns, letter combinations, or word endings and beginnings, just as you did when you tried to break the code in the example above. As code breakers spot patterns, they begin to uncover recognizable words and eventually they decode the text. Government codes tend to be complicated and require the code breakers to have advanced skills in decrypting, or cracking. As you can see, secret agent KIA, it's not easy to be a code breaker. But if you're good with details and like to figure things out, you may want to keep your codebook handy!

▶ According to the article, the science of secret communication is called _____

   A   code breaking

   B   cipher

   C   cryptology

   D   decrypting

Now that you cracked the code, use your knowledge to figure out the answer to the sample question using the **Know It All Approach.**

Start by reading the passage carefully. Underline the words that you think are the most interesting and important.

Then carefully read the question and the four answer choices.

What do you think about answer choice (A)? While code breaking is discussed in the passage, is it the name of the science of secret communication? Look back at the passage. *Code breaking* is the art of cracking codes. Answer choice (A) is not correct. Draw a line through answer choice (A).

What about answer choice (B)? The word *cipher* is mentioned in the passage. You may have underlined this word while reading. Look back at the passage. Cipher is defined as the system of transforming the text in order to conceal its meaning. Answer choice (B) is not correct.

What about answer choice (C)? The word *cryptology* appears in the passage. You may have underlined this word while reading. Look back to the passage. Cryptology is defined as the science of secret communication. This answer choice is a perfect match, but check out (D) before you make a final decision.

Look at answer choice (D). Is *decrypting* the name of the science of secret communication? Look back to the passage. Decrypting is the term for cracking codes. Answer choice (D) is not correct.

The **Know It All Approach** has helped you find the correct answer: answer choice (C). The correct answer choice has to be supported by information in the passage. Always use the information in the passage to identify the correct answer.

Ready to read some more passages and answer questions? On your mark, get set, GO!

Watch Her Go

It's July 1960, and you are a spectator at the Olympics in Rome, Italy. The 100-meter dash is in progress, and … the winner is Wilma Rudolph! Now the 200-meter dash is in progress, and the winner, faster than a speeding bullet, is Wilma Rudolph! Now, she's shooting across the finish line, bringing the women's relay team to victory in record-breaking time!

It was at the 1960 Olympics that Wilma Rudolph became the first American woman to earn three gold medals at a single Olympics. She also became known as the "world's fastest woman," but this running champion was not always on the fast track.

Wilma Rudolph spent the majority of her childhood in bed, sick with double pneumonia, scarlet fever, and later, polio. She became crippled from her illness, losing the use of her left leg, and had to be fitted with metal leg braces. With the help of a supportive family and her own determined spirit, Rudolph exercised her legs and pushed through physical therapy. By the age of nine, she was walking right out of her leg braces! Just a few years later, Rudolph became a basketball star in high school in Tennessee, leading her team to a state championship and setting state records for scoring. Abandoning basketball for track a short time later, Rudolph competed in her first Olympic Games at the age of sixteen and won a bronze medal. After high school, she enrolled at Tennessee State University, where she began preparing for the Olympic Games in Rome.

Off the track, Rudolph was setting records too. Her determination and skill broke barriers in previously all-male track and field events. She paved the way for African American athletes and was a great inspiration to people with physical disabilities. After retiring from track competition, Rudolph became a coach and later became a sports commentator on television and radio. She also started her own non-profit athletic outreach program, the Wilma Rudolph Foundation. Rudolph was only fifty-four when she died of cancer at her home in Nashville, Tennessee. A champion both on the track and off, her running shoes cannot be filled.

1. What happened right after Wilma Rudolph lost the use of her left leg?

    A   She was fitted with metal leg braces.
    B   She was sick with double pneumonia.
    C   She won a bronze metal in the relay.
    D   She became a coach and went into broadcasting.

2. What information supports the statement, "Off the track, Rudolph was setting records too"?

    A   She won the 100-meter dash in the 1960 Olympics.
    B   Her celebrity caused gender barriers to be broken.
    C   She was the first American woman to earn three gold medals at a single Olympics.
    D   She set the Olympic record for the 200-meter dash.

Where Did All of the Dinosaurs Go?

There is a lot of scientific debate over what caused the massive extinction of dinosaurs about 65 million years ago, at the end of the Cretaceous Period. Regardless of the controversy surrounding the great dinosaur disappearance, scientists generally agree upon the following points:

- 65 million years ago, Earth underwent a permanent, global climatic change.

- Temporary environmental changes occurred. These changes may have been the consequence of a major terrestrial, or earthly, disturbance. As a result of the disturbances, soot and dust darkened the sky and polluted the air, causing short-term acid rain, the release of poisonous gases, and global cooling.

- Many life forms aside from dinosaurs, including both land and marine organisms, went extinct. The climate change probably caused this extinction. Even if dinosaurs had survived the climate changes, it is likely they would not have had enough food to eat.

How do these three points relate to the extinction of the dinosaurs? Well, if the climate changed, the dinosaurs may not have been suited for the new climate. Acid rain and the release of poisonous gases most likely made it difficult for dinosaurs to breathe and exist. If there were not much for dinosaurs to feed on, they would starve!

While scientists may agree on the points mentioned above, they disagree about what caused these conditions to exist. What is clear is that in order for such changes to occur, a major event must have taken place. Some possibilities include a meteorite, comet, or an enormous asteroid striking Earth. Additional possibilities include a volcanic eruption, or changes in Earth's course or magnetic field. Although no one knows for sure why the dinosaurs disappeared, we do know that dinosaurs were around for a long time; they dominated the Earth for about 165 million years. That makes dinosaurs the longest living species on Earth. Who knows, maybe after all that time on Earth, they got bored and needed to find a new home!

3. What do scientists *disagree* on when it comes to the extinction of the dinosaurs?

    A   That permanent, global climatic changes occurred about 65 million years ago.
    B   That dinosaurs dominated Earth for about 165 million years.
    C   That temporary environmental changes occurred about 65 million years ago.
    D   What caused the climate change to take place about 65 million years ago.

4. According to the passage, the end of the Cretaceous Period was about how many years ago?

    A   165 million years ago
    B   60 million years ago
    C   65 million years ago
    D   230 million years ago

5. What three points do scientists agree on regarding the extinction of the dinosaurs and how do those points relate to the disappearance of dinosaurs? Support your answer with details from the passage.

    _____

    _____

    _____

    _____

    _____

    _____

Subject Review

Do you know how to spot details and supporting details? This chapter was full of details about secret messages, fast Olympians, and extinct dinosaurs, but it was also full of useful information to keep you on track.

Details are the facts and particulars that make articles, poems, and stories more interesting to read. They generally answer the questions: who, what, when, where, why, and how—the things you want to know on your journey to become a *know it all.*

Supporting details are facts and particulars that support the overall meaning of an article, poem, or story. They help you to learn more about a topic.

Now you should be able to answer the questions from the beginning of the chapter.

What does "mostabc peopleabc shedabc 45670 poundsabc ofabc skinabc inabc aabc lifetimeabc" mean?
Using the secret code disclosed in the passage, the code translates to "most people shed about 40 pounds of skin in a lifetime." Yuck! Be sure to clean up after your skin!

What title did Wilma Rudolph earn in 1960?
By winning three gold medals in the July,1960 Olympics, Wilma Rudolph earned the title, "the world's fastest woman."

What three events might have led to the extinction of the dinosaurs?
According to the passage in this chapter, a permanent, global climatic change 65 million years ago, temporary environmental changes, and the extinction of many life forms, including marine and terrestrial organisms, are the three events that scientist agree led to the extinction of dinosaurs.

Feeling adventurous? Not sure what to expect? Turn the page at your own risk ....

CHAPTER 3
Vocabulary in Context

What is a bacterial fart?

Which of the following is the best definition of a "Bikelophone" based on the passage?

A   the art of talking on the phone while riding a bike

B   a bike that comes with a phone built into its handlebars

C   a phone shaped like a bike that has a ring like a bike horn

D   an instrument configuration that produces a wide range of sounds

What is an SPF?

G et ready to play word detective as you learn about context clues in this chapter about vocabulary in context.

Context and Vocabulary

Context is the environment in which something exists. In a passage, context refers to words and sentences that surround a particular word or phrase. These surrounding words and sentences are helpful when you come across an unfamiliar word or phrase. By paying attention to surrounding words and sentences, or **context clues,** you can usually determine the meaning of the unfamiliar word or phrase.

Vocabulary in context refers to the meaning of a word or phrase based on the context in which it appears. Context clues, which include the sentence and paragraph in which the word or phrase appears, can help you to determine the meaning of unfamiliar words or phrases.

Read these tips. After you read them, journey into the *know it all* zone.

- Don't worry if the word or phrase that you are asked to define is completely unfamiliar to you. There will always be enough information in the passage to allow you to figure out a word's meaning.

- Make sure there is information in the passage to support the answer choice you select.

- When looking for context clues for a certain word in a long passage, you don't need to review the entire passage. Rather, focus on the paragraph and sentence in which the word appears. That's where you will find the clues you need to figure out the word's meaning.

- If you are not having much luck using context clues, look at the structure of the word or phrase. Is there anything about the word that is familiar to you, such as a prefix or a suffix?

Need some gas to rev up your engines? Read the following example to find out how to fill up!

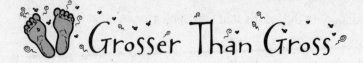
Grosser Than Gross

Hold Your Nose

There's a horrendous stench spreading through the room. Do you

A   pretend you don't smell anything unusual?

B   blame it on the dog?

C   make a big deal of the smell?

D   casually vanish from the room?

Yes, we are talking about farts, toots, smellies, cutting muffins. Whatever you call them, there is no disguising those unfortunate outbursts.

You may have noticed that certain foods, such as beans, make you gassy. The reason that beans cause gaseous after effects has to do with a family of sugars called *oligosaccharides.* It's no coincidence that other gassy foods, such as onions, soybeans, cabbage, and peas, are also naturally sweetened by oligosaccharides. These complex sugars are bulky, gawky molecules that are too large to creep into your body through the lining of your small intestine. Therefore, oligosaccharides travel through the small intestine and enter the large intestine, still carrying important nutrients. The bacteria in your large intestine devour the nutrients. As they chow down the complex sugars, they create gas. Your body must release it as bacterial farts!

Do you think all farts are the same? Think again. Farts come in many varieties. For the most part, gas itself is odorless; it is the food we eat that creates a smell. Sulfur-rich foods such as cauliflower, eggs, and meat tend to produce stinky farts. Beans generate farts that are not particularly smelly. The foul news: most people fart an average of fourteen times a day!

▶ What is an *oligosaccharide*?

A   a gassy food

B   a bacterial fart

C   a complex sugar

D   a bacteria in your intestines

Now that you've let loose a bit, figure out the answer to the sample question. Using the **Know It All Approach**.

Start by reading the passage carefully. Underline the words that you think are the most interesting and important.

Then carefully read the question and all of the four answer choices.

What do you think about answer choice (A)? While the passage mentions a number of gassy foods, does it mention that oligosaccharides are *gassy foods*? Look back at the passage. The passage states that a number of gassy foods "are naturally sweetened with a family of sugars called oligosaccharides," but oligosaccharides are not listed as gassy foods. Answer choice (A) is not correct.

What about answer choice (B)? Are oligosaccharides another name for *a bacterial fart*? The passage explains that as the bacteria in your large intestine gulp in the complex sugars, they let out gas, or bacterial farts. Answer choice (B) is not correct.

What about answer choice (C)? Are oligosaccharides *complex sugars*? Take a look back at the passage. The passage notes that some gassy foods "are naturally sweetened with a family of sugars called oligosaccharide." It then goes on to discuss the fate of the *complex sugars*. By using the context clues, you can determine that oligosaccharides are complex sugars. Before you make your final choice, look at the remaining answer choice. You should always be sure that you are selecting the best answer.

What about answer choice (D)? Are oligosaccharides *bacteria in your intestines*? The passage explains that as bacteria in your intestine "gulp in the complex sugars they let out gas, which are actually bacterial farts." Answer choice (D) is wrong.

The **Know It All Approach** has helped you find the correct answer: answer choice (C). The context clues in the passage support your answer. Always be sure to use only information from the passage to answer questions and to read all of the answer choices. You never know when you will find a better answer further down the page!

Now make a different kind of noise reading these passages and questions.

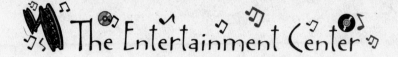
The Entertainment Center

Strange Sounds

If you listen to rock music, or if you've watched a sci-fi or horror movie from the 1950s, chances are you have heard a *theremin*. It's a musical instrument whose creepy sound effects bring you to the edge of your seat. Invented by Lev Termen around 1920, the theremin is one of the first electronic instruments. It is equipped with two antennas, which create a surrounding magnetic field. One antenna controls pitch; the other controls volume. No physical contact is made between the player and the instrument, sound and pitch are controlled by the player's hands moving within the magnetic field. While it's a very innovative creation, the theremin is not the only **uncanny** musical instrument out there.

When you think of a bike, you think of travel, right? Think again! The *bikelophone* is an instrument with a **configuration** of bike parts, magnetic pieces, a mechanical foot pedal, a tone generator, scrap wood and metal, bass strings, telephone bells, and metal bowls. The magnetic pieces amplify, or intensify, the bikelophone's sounds. Invented by Stephen Schweitzer as a side instrument for a band, the bikelophone makes both soothing and terrifying sounds and takes your ears for a wild ride!

Inspired to make your own sounds? With a little imagination and a few random objects, you can create your own weird instrument. When the noise begins to irritate your family and friends, though, just don't let them know where the idea came from!

1. Which of the following is the best definition of the word *uncanny* in the first paragraph's phrase "**uncanny** musical instruments"?

   A   peculiar
   B   boring
   C   normal
   D   classic

2. In the second paragraph, what does the word *configuration* mean?

   A   sound
   B   generator
   C   range
   D   arrangement

Mad Science

To Burn or Not to Burn

Have you ever wondered what "sun protection factor," or SPF, really means? How does sunblock actually "block" the Sun's intense ultraviolet rays? To begin with, SPF describes the amount of time of sun exposure it takes before your particular skin type burns. This time is your minimal erythemal dose, or MED. How do you tell your MED? You can stay out in the Sun and **clock** the minutes until your skin begins to tingle and burn.

You can also estimate based on statistics. Light-skinned people tend to have an MED of approximately ten minutes. People with medium to darker skin tend to have an MED of about fifteen minutes. Based on both your MED and the SPF, or how much protection you're given from the Sun, you can calculate how long you'll be protected before burning. If you're wearing a sunscreen with SPF 15 and your MED is 10 minutes, you are protected for 150 minutes (15 times 10 equals 150). If you want to stay out in the Sun for 225 minutes with protection and your MED is fifteen minutes, you would wear SPF 15 (15 times 15 equals 225). Remember the two golden rules of SPF: if you feel yourself burning, run for cover. If you take a dip in the pool or ocean, reapply your SPF and let the countdown begin again!

How do manufacturers of sunscreens guarantee that their lotions are really the SPF they claim them to be? They rely on scientists to help with their final testing stage. Scientists find testees and make an appointment for each testee to experience the "solar simulator." This machine consists of a xenon bulb whose **concentrated** ultraviolet and visible light can create a sunburn faster than you can say *summertime is fun time*!

Each testee undergoes the force of the solar simulator to determine his or her personal MED. Then, on each testee's back, a small square of skin is marked off and smeared with the sunscreen supplied by a sunscreen manufacturer. The solar simulator zaps the testee's sunscreen patch in a line of small circles. The sunbeam simulator **irradiates** each spot for a varying amount of time. It shines on some spots shorter, some longer than the goal time. Twenty-four hours later, if there's at least one spot below the intended SPF that remains milky and at least one spot above the estimated SPF that has burned, bingo!

3. Read this sentence from the passage.

"You can stay out in the Sun and **clock** the minutes until your flesh begins to turn pink, or you can estimate…"

In this sentence, what does *clock* mean?

A   chronometer
B   timepiece
C   alarm clock
D   observe

4. Which of the following is the best definition of the word *irradiates* in the third paragraph?

A   shines
B   spots
C   targets
D   presses

5. Read this sentence from the passage.

"This device holds a xenon bulb that pumps out **concentrated** ultraviolet and visible light that can deliver a sunburn in a matter of minutes."

Use information in the passage to explain what *concentrated* means.

_____

_____

_____

_____

Subject Review

Can you determine the meanings of words using context clues? Do you know that the meaning of a word may vary according to the context in which it appears? This chapter was full of unusual smells and sounds, but it also shed light on some useful information.

By paying attention to surrounding words and sentences, or *context clues*, you can usually determine the meaning of the unfamiliar word or phrase.

Vocabulary in context refers to the meaning of a word or phrase based on the context in which it appears.

Now you should be able to answer the questions from the beginning of the chapter.

What is a bacterial fart?

A bacterial fart is the gas released from your body when the bacteria in your large intestine devour valuable nutrients found in oligosaccharides.

Which of the following is the best definition of a bikelophone based on the passage?

A the art of talking on the phone while riding a bike

B a bike that comes with a phone built into its handlebars

C a phone shaped like a bike that has a ring like a bike horn

D an instrument configuration that produces a wide range of sounds

The correct answer is (D), an instrument configuration that produces a wide range of sounds.

What is an SPF?

An SPF, or sun protection factor, indicates how many minutes you can stay out in the Sun without burning.

Ready to venture forth? Carry on then. May the *Know It All!* force be with you.

CHAPTER 4
Fact and Opinion

Which of the following is a fact?

A   Canada is the only country with triskaidekaphobes.

B   Triskaidekaphobes fear the number thirteen.

C   People who fear the number thirteen live in Italy.

D   Triskaidekaphobes are crazy!

Fact or opinion: An albatross can sleep while flying.

Which of the following is an opinion?

A   Bollywood movies attempt to appeal to everyone in India.

B   Bollywood is the official center of Indian film.

C   Bollywood movies average two-and-a-half hours.

D   Bollywood is better than Hollywood.

amed novelist Mark Twain once said, Get your facts first, the you can distort them as much as you please. Get your facts straight in this chapter about fact and opinion.

Facts and Opinions

Statements of fact can be proved to be true by a dictionary or encyclopedia, by direct examination, or by an expert. Facts have objective reality, which means that whether or not we agree with them, they are true.

Statements of opinion simply tell how a person feels. Opinions are the views or judgments that form in your mind about a particular matter.

When answering **Fact Questions**

- Look for specific details from the passages

- Label paragraphs

- Skim for key words

When answering **Opinion Questions**

- Remember that opinions are details that cannot be found in a dictionary or encyclopedia

- Keep in mind that opinions reflect views or judgments

When answering **Open-Response Opinion Questions**

- Be sure to answer the question that is being asked

- State your opinion clearly

- Use examples from the selection to support your opinion

Superstitious? Check out the example on the next page. Good luck!

Why Are People Afraid of a Number?

Even if it's sheer coincidence, the number thirteen sure has some interesting events associated with it. The number thirteen's unlucky identity goes far back in history.

According to Norse mythology, the war god Odin invited eleven of his dearest friends to a party; including himself, the party made twelve. Loki, the god of evil and turmoil, crashed the party, being the thirteenth guest. As the story goes, one of the most beloved gods, Balder, who also happened to be Odin's son, tried to make the trouble-making Loki leave the party. An unruly quarrel ensued, which resulted in the death of precious Balder. The number thirteen was certainly not a lucky number for Odin!

Who else fears the number thirteen? Well, some Christians believe the number thirteen is unlucky because there were thirteen people at the Last Supper. More recently, it was on April 13, 1970, that the Apollo 13 entered the moon's gravitational field, when its oxygen tank exploded. Fortunately, the Apollo 13 made a successful return to Earth!

According to Thomas J. Fernsler, a mathematics policy scientist, people may fear the number thirteen because of its position after the "complete" number twelve. What makes a number "complete"? Well, consider these facts regarding the number twelve: twelve months make up a year, the zodiac consists of twelve signs, there were twelve tribes of ancient Israel, and the number of apostles to Jesus was twelve. According to Fernsler, the bad fortune of the number thirteen is that it seems "restless" or chaotic because it falls after the "complete" number twelve.

Have you ever stayed on the thirteenth floor in a hotel? If not, it may be because the floor numbers of many hotels and skyscrapers go from the twelfth floor to the fourteenth floor, and there is no thirteenth floor! Those fearful of the number thirteen exist outside of the United States too. Apparently, thirteen's unluckiness got around. Would you believe that the number thirteen is not included in Italy's national lottery? People in France also have issues regarding the number thirteen. Some fearful-of-thirteen French went so far as to create an organization that supplies last minute dinner guests in case a host realizes that thirteen people are expected to dinner.

▶ Which of the following details in this passage is a fact?

A   People fear the number thirteen because it comes after the number twelve.

B   Everything associated with the number twelve is good.

C   People in France fear the number thirteen more than people in Italy.

D   An explosion on April 13 occurred on the Apollo 13 mission.

Now that you know what the number thirteen hype is all about, use your knowledge to figure out the answer to the sample question.

Start by reading the passage carefully. Underline the words that you think are the most interesting and important.

Then carefully read the question and all of the four answer choices.

What do you think about answer choice (A)? Is this a fact from the article or is it an opinion? Would you find this statement in a dictionary or encyclopedia? Most likely, you would not. Answer choice (A) is not correct.

What about answer choice (B)? Is this a fact from the article or is it an opinion? Some people might not think that everything associated with the number 12 is good. You would not find this statement in a dictionary or encyclopedia. Answer choice (B) is not correct.

What about answer choice (C)? Is this a fact from the article or is it an opinion? Would you be able to find information to prove this statement was true in a dictionary or encyclopedia? Most likely you would not be able to. Answer choice (C) is not correct.

Look at answer choice (D). Is this a fact from the article or is it an opinion? Would you be able to find to verify if an explosion on April 13 struck the Apollo 13 mission? You would. An encyclopedia would contain this information. Therefore, answer choice (D) is correct.

The **Know It All Approach** has helped you find the correct answer: answer choice (D). The correct answer choice has to be supported by information in the passage. Always use the information in the passage to identify the correct answer.

Now tune into the next passages and questions.

Alternative Animals

Willie's Weird and Wonderful Animal Facts

"Welcome to the after-school network. We are live with, Willie Ramos, nature reporter for our Weird and Wonderful Animal Fact segment. Willie, what tales of truth do you have to share?"

"Right now, I am watching a chameleon. They can move their eyes in two different directions at the same time!"

"Are you sure about that Willie? Maybe your eyes are just playing tricks on you."

"I'm sure, alright. Mr. Verdad, a fact-finding fanatic, has accompanied me on my latest discovery mission."

"Back to you then, Willie, don't keep us in suspense!"

"Check this out: A cockroach can live for up to a week without a head! How awesome would it be if we could leave our heads at home for a week while our bodies went to school?"

"Just give us the facts, Willie!"

"Right. Okay. Did you know that only female mosquitoes bite? In order to produce mosquito eggs, females need protein from blood. Getting bit by mosquitoes sucks!"

"We seem to have lost the connection, folks. Willie, you still there? Willie?"

"I'm here alright! Mr. Verdad and I were just watching an albatross flying up above. What's that Mr. Verdad? Wow! I just learned that an albatross can snooze while flying. It can catch zzz's while cruising at twenty-five miles per hour! I wouldn't mind sleeping while I was riding my bike to school."

"What was that last comment, Willie? I didn't hear you."

"Uh, nothing. I was just watching some lovebirds."

"Lovebirds…I once had lovebirds. Why don't you tell everyone what lovebirds are, Willie?"

"Sure. They're small parakeets that live in pairs. Gosh, it's hard to tell them apart; they both look so much alike. Hold on a minute … Mr. Verdad just told me that male lovebirds have brighter colors than the females."

"Thanks for your totally awesome updates, Willie! That's all we have time for today on our Weird and Wonderful Animal Fact segment. Tune in next week for more fun facts!"

1. Which of the following is an opinion in the passage?

    A   A cockroach can live for up to a week without a head.
    B   An albatross can sleep while flying.
    C   Getting bit by mosquitoes sucks.
    D   Male lovebirds have brighter colors than the females.

2. Write a list of the facts about birds from this passage.

_____

_____

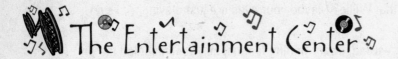

The Other Hollywood

In America, the center of the film world is Hollywood, but did you know that Bollywood—the hub of Indian film located in Bombay—produces twice as many films each year as Hollywood? If you were contemplating an acting career, perhaps you should consider checking out what Bollywood has to offer.

Before you venture to Bollywood to achieve fame; however, you may want to consider the differences between Hollywood and Bollywood films. Unlike Hollywood movies, Bollywood movies pack in numerous sing-along dance numbers. No matter the genre—be it a sentimental love story or a gritty crime drama—there's a good chance the characters are going to burst into song. If you want to make it in Bollywood, you better brush up on your dance moves. A few singing lessons wouldn't hurt either.

Another downside is the long hours. Many Hollywood blockbusters run about an hour and a half long. By contrast, the average Bollywood movies clocks in at two-and-a-half hours. For the would-be Bollywood star this means spending more time rehearsing movie scenes.

If you crave innovative and unusual roles to play, you may be disappointed with Bollywood's scripts. While Bollywood's movies tend to be vibrant, romantic, and cheerful, they are also be formulaic. Bollywood movies often focus on a central love story, usually involving to good lovers from different social classes. Add in some stereotypical villains and a few song and dance numbers and you've got a Bollywood hit.

Despite the longer hours and all the fancy footwork, there is one undeniable advantage to a career in Bollywood films. While Hollywood actors are often in and out of the spotlight as fast as you can say New Kids On The Block, once a Bollywood actor achieves celebrity status, they are in the spotlight for the long haul. Famous faces are the bread and butter of Bollywood and actors work as often as they can. There are stories of Bollywood actors working on 100 films at the same time! In Hollywood, doing a couple of films in the same year is big deal.

Whether you choose Hollywood or Bollywood, hope to see your name up in lights!

3. Which of the following is a fact in the passage?

   A There are stories of actors working on over 100 films simultaneously.
   B Bollywood produces twice as many films each year as Hollywood.
   C You would spend more time rehearsing movie scenes in Bollywood.
   D You may be disappointed with Bollywood's movie scripts.

4. Which of the following is **not** a fact in the passage?

   A Bollywood movies are an average of two-and-a-half hours long.
   B Bollywood movies have at least five sing-along dance routines each.
   C If you want to be famous, then Bollywood maybe just the right place for you.
   D Bollywood movies attempt to appeal to everyone in India.

5. Write a list of opinions found in this passage.

   _____

   _____

   _____

Subject Review

Are you clear on fact versus opinion? This chapter was full of number stories, animal trivia, and routes to stardom, but it was also full of useful information.

Facts are statements of fact can be proved true by a dictionary or encyclopedia, by direct examination, or by an expert.

Opinions, unlike facts, tell how a person feels. Opinions cannot be proved true or false. Opinions are the views or judgments that form in your mind about a particular matter.

Now you should be able to answer the questions from the beginning of the chapter.

Which of the following is a fact?

A Canada is the only country with triskaidekaphobes.

B Triskaidekaphobes fear the number thirteen.

C People who fear the number thirteen live in Italy.

D Triskaidekaphobes are crazy!

The answer is (B) Triskaidekaphobes fear the number thirteen.

Fact or opinion: An albatross can sleep while flying.
Fact! An albatross can sleep while flying. It can catch some shut-eye cruising at 25 miles per hour.

Which of the following is an opinion?

A Bollywood movies attempt to appeal to everyone in India.

B Bollywood is the official center of Indian film.

C Bollywood movies average two-and-a-half hours.

D Bollywood is better than Hollywood.

The answer is (D), Bollywood is better than Hollywood. Folks in Hollywood may think Hollywood is better than Bollywood!

Hip History

Top Story

Whether you sleep in it, play sports in it, bum around the house in it, or wear it with your favorite jeans, chances are there's a story behind your favorite T-shirt. It's hard to imagine a time in which T-shirts didn't exist, but as recently as a few decades ago, T-shirts served quite a different purpose than they do today—that is, they were considered to be underwear! That was before T-shirts be were used to advertise brands, bands, and teams. Nowadays, T-shirts are an important advertising tool.

T-shirts made its debut as a part of a military uniform. Americans first encountered the T-shirt during World War I. Dressed in wool uniforms, many American soldiers dreaded the hot European summer. While the Americans sweated out the hot days, European soldiers were cool in their lightweight cotton undershirts. It wasn't long before the American troops figured it out. They abandoned their heavy garments and began to wear T-shirts, too. Return troops brought the T-shirts back home with them and, by the 1920s, the garment was common enough to make into the *Merriam-Websters Dictionary*. Still, it was considered an undergarment and still most common in military circles. In World War II, the T-shirt was the standard under garment for both the Navy and the Army.

Throughout the 1950s the T-shirt made the slow trip from undergarment to outerwear. Movie and television celebrities wore them in popular films like *The Wild One* and *Rebel Without a Cause*. By the 1960s, the T-shirt was the shirt of choice for the young crowd. Inexpensive, and stylish, too, T-shirts were the perfect way to express yourself. T-shirts screen-printed with rock 'n' roll band names, company logos, or political slogans provided people with an easy and comfortable way to advertise themselves to the world.

Today most of us consider T-shirts a staple in our wardrobes. Comfortable, casual, and always in style, T-shirts are tops above the rest.

I got all the answers right and all I got was this **lousy** T-shirt

1. According to the passage, when did the word T-shirt appear in the *Merriam–Webster's Dictionary*?

   A   by the 1920s
   B   by the 1960s
   C   by the 1980s
   D   by the 1990s

2. In paragraph 2, the word *debut* means

   A   last statement
   B   first appearance
   C   farewell
   D   offering

3. Which of the following is a fact from the passage?

   A   Everyone wears T-shirts.
   B   T-shirts are inexpensive tops.
   C   The T-shirt first appeared during World War I.
   D   The T-shirt is a great product.

4. Write a list of the opinions in this article.

   _____

   _____

   _____

   _____

   _____

5. Do you think the invention of the T-shirt was important? Support your answer with examples from the story.

   _____

   _____

   _____

   _____

   _____

CHAPTER 5
Main Idea, Summary, and Theme

Which of the following statements best summarize Orson Welles's radio broadcast of his adaptation of <u>The War of the Worlds</u>?

A   It was so realistic that nationwide people panicked.

B   People tuned out because they were bored with the radio play.

C   Martians loved it so much that they landed in New York.

D   People listening in decided to become Martians.

How many sumo wrestlers are there in the continental United States?

How many Academy Awards has the cartoon <u>Tom and Jerry</u> won?

Ready to for more? Cut to the chase and get to the point by completing this chapter about main idea, summary, and theme.

The **main idea** is the key point or more important idea in passage, or the portion of the passage that you are asked to consider. Most stories and articles that you read will have a main idea or essential message, along with supporting details that explain and demonstrate the main idea. The main idea may be explicitly stated within a passage or it may be suggested by information in a passage.

Here are some tips to help you tackle questions about the main idea.

- For multiple-choice questions that ask you to determine the main idea of a passage, make sure your answer summarizes the entire passage and not just a portion of it.

- For open-response questions that ask you to identify the main idea, be sure that you find details from the passage to support your answer. Keep your answer focused.

A **summary** covers the main points in a concise, brief manner. A summary, like an outline, notes only the key features or parts of a story, poem, novel, play, or article. A summary can serve as a preview or recap of what you have read.

If you're taking a test and are asked a summary question, keep these tips in mind.

- For multiple-choice questions that ask you to summarize what you have read, be sure that the information supplied is in the right order and that all of the main points of the passage are included.

- For open-response questions that ask you to write a summary, be sure to include a sentence for each of the main ideas and to include a few details—just enough to make the main ideas clear. Be sure to read your summary after you are finished writing it. Is the information in the right order? Does it all make sense?

The **theme** is the central message of a story, poem, novel, play, or article that readers can apply to life. Some works have a stated theme, which is expressed directly. More commonly, works have an implied theme, which is revealed gradually. Implied themes are something the reader has to work out for themselves using clues the writer has given.

These two tips should help you tackle questions regarding themes.

- For multiple-choice questions that ask you to identify the theme of a passage, make sure your answer expresses the central message of what you have read.

- For open-response questions that ask you to discuss the theme of what you have read be sure to include details to support your answer.

Now read this passage about one of the greatest hoaxes of all time. Then, try the sample questions on the next page.

 Art-rageous

Martians Go Home!

On October 30, 1938, a Martian spaceship landed on a New Jersey farm. Reporters, police officers, and curious New Jersey residents flocked to the scene. But curiosity quickly gave way to terror as the Martians revealed their hostile intentions and attacked. Soon, other ships landed and the Martian invasion was underway.

Sound far-fetched? It didn't to the millions of American radio listeners who tuned in that night. What most of the listeners at home did not know was that the Martian landing, and the invasion that followed, was a fake! The whole thing was staged by Orson Welles, a famous film director, and his Mercury Theater of the Air, a group of radio actors who broadcast plays over the radio. On the night before Halloween, the Mercury Theater presented an adaptation of H. G. Wells's classic *The War of the Worlds*. To update the story and add to the dramatic impact, they presented their tale as a series of newsflashes. Because they had an American audience, the scriptwriters moved the story from England to America. The various actors took the roles of reporters and Washington officials. Between the fake newsbreaks, a musical program "already in progress" was used as a filler. Listeners who tuned in from the very beginning heard a brief explanation of the night's play, but for anyone who tuned in late, it sounded like America was under attack by Martians.

The pretend news broadcasts caused a panic. Many listeners believed that the Martians had actually invaded and were out to destroy New York and New Jersey. Confused and fear-stricken listeners all over the country either fled their homes or hid out in cellars. Some armed themselves, ready to do battle with the alien foe. Others, taking the fantastic description of the Martians' poison gas weapons for reality, wrapped wet towels around their heads for protection.

Genuine news outlets quickly reported on the widespread panic. As a result of the scandal, Orsen Welles was forced to issue a statement of apology to the public. Furthermore, the Columbia Broadcasting System (CBS), which broadcasted the Mercury Theater of the Air, announced they would never again broadcast imaginary news reports that had the potential to disturb listeners. This means that if ever you are tuning in and hear about a Martian invasion over the air, chances are that it's not a hoax—run!

Chapter 5 • Main Idea, Summary, and Theme

▶ What is the main idea of this passage?

A   Martians invaded New York and New Jersey on October 30,1938.
B   Some radio programs like to scare their listeners to improve ratings.
C   Entertainment can lead to mass hysteria if people mistake it for real.
D   Martians can invade at the most unlikely times—we need to be prepared.

▶ Write a summary of this passage. Support your answer with details and specific information from the passage.

_____

_____

_____

_____

Now that you've ventured into the twilight zone, take a trip back to reality and figure out the answer to the sample question.

First, look at how to answer the multiple-choice question. Start by reading the passage carefully. Underline the words that you think are the most interesting and important.

Then, carefully read the question and all four answer choices.

What do you think about answer choice (A)? The question asks you to find the main idea. Did Martians invade New York and New Jersey? Look back at the passage. Answer choice (A) is not correct; the passage is not about Martians invading New York or New Jersey.

What about answer choice (B)? Does it state the main idea of the passage? Look back at the passage. Answer choice (B) is not correct; the passage is not about radio programs that like to scare their listeners.

What about answer choice (C)? Does it state the main idea of the passage? Look back at the passage. The passage is about how something that was meant to entertain audiences resulted in mass hysteria because the listeners believed it was real. Answer choice (C) is most likely the correct answer. But, read the remaining answer choices before you before you choose your final answer.

What about answer choice (D)? Does it state the main idea of the passage? No! The passage is not about Martians invading at unlikely times. Answer choice (D) is not correct.

The correct answer is answer is (C).

The **Know It All Approach** has helped you find the correct answer: answer choice (C). The correct answer choice has to be supported by information in the passage. Always use the information in the passage to identify the correct answer.

Now, try the open-response question. Again, start by reading the passage carefully. Underline the words that you think are the most interesting and important.

Then carefully read the question. Be sure that you are clear on what the question is asking you. In this case, you are being asked to write a summary of the passage, using details and specific information from the passage.

Before you begin writing, plan your answer. Return to the passage and look at your notes in the margins or any words that you may have underlined. In writing your summary, be sure to use only the information provided in the passage in your answer.

Once you start writing, be sure to write your answer neatly and clearly.

- Here is a sample answer to the open-response question.

People listening to a popular radio program in 1938 were fooled by a play that the station was broadcasting. Nationwide, listeners believed that Martians were invading. The reason many listeners were fooled was because they missed explanations at the beginning of the program and 40 minutes into it that explained that people were listening to a play. People became hysterical from the broadcast—they hid in cellars, loaded guns, even wrapped their heads in wet towels as protection from Martian poison gas, in an attempt to defend themselves against aliens. The network that broadcast the play later apologized and promised that it would not air a news broadcast that might scare listeners.

After writing your answer, read the question and your answer again. Does the paragraph above summarize the information you read in the passage? Look back at the passage. The paragraph does list the main ideas of the passage. It includes some details from the passage as well.

Finally, check your answer for any errors in punctuation, spelling, usage, or grammar.

Congratulations! You are ready to move on! Remember to refer back to these pages if you need help with answering multiple-choice or open-response questions.

Now, get into the ring and let the fun begin! Unless you are a lightweight, of course!

 Extreme Sports

Heavy Weights

Up until the beginning of the 1990s, sumo wrestling was virtually unknown in the United States. Its appearance in the 1990s is due mainly to wrestling promoter and judo instructor Yoshisada Yonezuka, who grew up sumo wrestling in Japan. In 1992, Japanese sumo officials enlisted the help of Yonezuka to help promote sumo in the United States. Sumo wrestling is a traditional Japanese sport dating back to the fifteenth century, but it has achieved limited popularity outside of its native country. When Japanese sumo officials approached Yonezuka, they hoped to increase the sport's international popularity in order and get of sumo wrestling included in future Olympic Games. Yonezuka, who already had a judo club in New Jersey, added sumo lessons to list of courses he offers.

Yonezuka began with one sumo student, Emanuel Yarbrough. Yarbrough, a 720-pound former college football player, was nationally ranked in judo and was a good candidate for sumo. After only three days of practicing sumo, Yarbrough came in second in the sumo world championships! In 1995, he was named the amateur world sumo champion.

To American audiences, who are unused to the sport, sumo is often misunderstood. To the uninitiated, it appears like a test of brute force. Two large men banging bellies and, in a matter of seconds, it is all over. But Japanese onlookers know how much skill it takes to be in the ring. Wrestlers in Japan immerse themselves in sumo. For champion wrestlers, sumo is a way of life. They live in their training facilities and practice wrestling throughout the day, every day. This level of commitment is almost unheard of in America, where wrestlers generally come to the sport after they are past a college football or wrestling career. Still, American wrestlers make up in size and strength, what they lack in tradition and skill.

Today, there are less than one hundred sumo wrestlers in the continental United States. But this is likely to change. Sumo clubs and tournaments have been appearing on both the east and west coasts. Those who are in the grips of sumo wrestling are optimistic that the sport will be a part of the 2012 or 2016 Olympics. This means that there's still plenty of time for you to bulk up, and get in the ring and try it!

1. What is the main idea of this passage?

   A   Sumo wrestling in Japan is more fun than sumo wrestling in America.
   B   Japanese sumo wrestlers train more than American sumo wrestlers.
   C   Sumo wrestling is just beginning to become visible as a sport in America.
   D   Sumo wrestling most likely will not make it into the 2012 Olympics.

2. Which of the following statements best summarize the third paragraph from the passage?

   A   Sumo wrestlers in Japan train intensely for the sport while sumo wrestlers in America often turn to the sport after they are finished with other sports careers.
   B   People in America don't understand sumo wrestling in Japan because they see the sport as two large men bumping bellies.
   C   American sumo wrestlers know that the sport is all about their size and strength and therefore do not spend a lot of time training.
   D   American wrestlers are older and therefore they don't care about going professional with sumo wrestling.

3. What is the theme of this passage? Use information from the passage to support your answer.

   _____

   _____

   _____

When reading passages, try these active reading tips.

- As you read, label each paragraph with its main idea. Paragraph labels can help you to identify the main idea, and to find the theme of a passage. Paragraph labels are also helpful when you need to summarize a passage. They can help you to note the order in which information appears in a passage.

- Don't get bogged down with the minor details in a passage. Don't try to memorize details as you read. You can always return to the passage when you answer questions.

Cat and Mouse Tales

Tom and Jerry, the cartoon world's most famous cat and mouse duo, were created in 1940 by the animation team of William Hanna and Joseph Barbera. Hanna, a New Mexico native, was studying to be an engineer when financial consideration forced him to quit his studies. His art talents landed him a job at an animation studio. Barbera, a New York native, lost his job as an accountant during the Great Depression. He eventually found work as a cartoonist. In 1938, Hanna and Barbera started working together at MGM's new animation studio in Hollywood.

At the time, MGM had no star characters, like Disney's Mickey Mouse or Warner Brothers's Bugs Bunny. To rectify this situation, Hanna and Barbera set out to make a cartoon stars MGM could call their own. They started with two characters Barbera had worked on at a previous studio: a pair of humans called Tom and Jerry. These original characters were changed into a cat and mouse. A cat and a mouse team made writing stories easy, because cats and mice were natural antagonists. When has a cat ever needed a reason to chase a mouse? All that was left for Hanna and Barbera was to create just the right cat and mouse for the chasing silliness to begin.

The first *Tom and Jerry* cartoon was not, technically, even a *Tom and Jerry* cartoon. Called "Puss Gets the Boot," the movie featured a cat named Jasper. Jasper spent the film unsuccessfully trying to catch an unnamed mouse. MGM didn't think the cartoon was very good, but they released it anyway. To MGM's shock, the public loved Jasper and the mouse! That year, "Puss Gets the Boot" received an Academy Award nomination for best animated short film!

Hanna and Barbera went on to make more than 100 cat and mouse cartoons, creating one crazy chase scene after the next for nearly two decades. *Tom and Jerry* cartoons met with great success: they went on to win seven Academy Awards!

The series ended in 1958 because of financial issues at MGM. However, Hanna and Barbera did not want to call it quits. When Hanna and Barbera started out in animation, cartoons were made to be shown on the big screen in movie theaters. Before a feature film would start, audiences got to watch a short cartoon. However, by the time *Tom and Jerry* was discontinued, a new medium had replaced movies as the main source of American entertainment: television.

Starting their own studio, Hanna and Barbera produced cartoons specifically tailored for television audiences. Working in this new medium, they created such famous cartoons as *The Flintstones, The Jetsons, Yogi Bear,* and *Scooby Doo.* Apparently, Hanna and Barbera learned something from their famous cat and mouse: you have to keep chasing your dreams, no matter how much they slip out of your reach.

4. What is the main idea of the passage? Use information from the article to support your answer.

_____

_____

_____

_____

_____

5. What is the main idea of the third paragraph?

A   You can never anticipate what the public will like.
B   The people who ran MGM were not very smart.
C   Hanna and Barbera knew exactly what they were doing.
D   Cat and mouse tales will always be favorites for viewers.

6. Which of the following statements best summarize the passage?

A   Hanna and Barbera were animators who created many successful cartoons.
B   *Tom and Jerry* was the only cartoon to win Academy Awards.
C   The best way to name cartoon characters is to pull names out of a hat.
D   Financial constraints at companies can force them to have to let go of their top employees.

7. Which of the following statements best expresses the theme of the passage?

A   Don't listen to the advice of your bosses.
B   Cat and mouse tales are what the public wants.
C   Cartoons can win Academy Awards.
D   Success often strikes when it is least expected.

Subject Review

Have you mastered how to recognize the main idea and theme and how to summarize things you read? This chapter was full of mock Martian invasions, wrestling sumo style, and a famous cat and mouse chase, but it was also full of useful information.

The main idea summarizes information in the entire passage, or the portion of the passage that you are asked to consider. The main idea may be explicitly stated within a passage or it may be suggested by information in a passage.

A summary covers the main points in a concise, brief manner. A summary, like an outline, notes only the key features or parts of a story, poem, novel, play, or article.

The theme is the central message of a story, poem, novel, play, or article that readers can apply to life.

Now you should be able to answer the questions from the beginning of the chapter.

Which of the following statements best summarize Orson Welles's radio broadcast of his adaptation of The War of the Worlds?

A It was so realistic that people nationwide panicked.

B People tuned out because they were bored with the radio play.

C Martians loved it so much that they landed in New York.

D People listening in decided to become Martians.

The answer is (A). It was so realistic that nationwide people panicked.

How many sumo wrestlers are there in the continental United States?

There are less than 100 sumo wrestlers in the continental United States.

How many Academy Awards has the cartoon Tom and Jerry won?

Well, a cartoon character can't win an Academy Award, but seven *Tom and Jerry* cartoons have won an Academy Award.

CHAPTER 6
Inferences

How did Sylvia Robinson know that the Sugarhill Gang would be a successful group?

It's likely that baseball-sewing experts

A   have a lot of patience.

B   are not detail oriented.

C   play pro baseball.

D   have sticky hands.

What changed for Zena once she graduated from high school?

Know it alls predict that you will get smarter by completing this chapter about inference. By the time you're through, we're sure you'll have come to the same conclusion.

Inferences

An **inference** requires that you use your reason and experience to come up with an idea, based on what an author implies or suggests. Inferences should be based on supporting details from the text you are reading as well as your own knowledge. If you read a story in which the author suggests that she is very excited about her birthday and within the story she walks into her house and everyone screams "Surprise!" you may infer that the author walked in on her surprise birthday party.

A **conclusion** is a general statement you can make and explain with reasoning, or with supporting details from a text. If you read a story in which a girl says that her pet Buddy purred so loud that she couldn't get to sleep the night before, you may conclude that her pet is a cat.

A **prediction** is a guess what will happen next. When you predict, you are drawing an inference. If you read a story in which a girl is practicing the cello every day, you may predict that she has a concert coming up.

A **generalization** is an inference that can apply to more than one item or group. A generalization has a more general scope than a prediction or a conclusion. If you read a story in which two brothers and their three cousins play musical instruments, you might generalize that they come from a musical family.

Got that all straight? Good. Now get in the groove by checking out this example.

Hip History

The Sugarhill Gang

Rap is truly an international phenomenon. In the United States, rappers regularly top the bestselling album charts. Rappers cut records from Mexico to France, from the United Kingdom to Japan. Rap performers and fans come from every racial group and all walks of life. But it wasn't always so. Rap began as an obscure underground music performed mainly in the boroughs of New York City. How did this musical style turn into one of the biggest culture movements since rock and roll? The Sugarhill Gang happened, that's what.

The Sugarhill Gang consisted of rap musicians Wonder Mike, Big Bank Hank, and Master Gee. In 1979, these three rappers changed the face to popular culture by releasing "Rapper's Delight." Their song, which featured a catchy sample beat and simple, sometimes humorous, lyrics, was not the first rap song, nor, as many critics point out, was it the best rap song ever made. But "Rapper's Delight" did what no rap song before could ever do: it broke into the Top 40 charts. When "Rapper's Delight" went big time, the entire rap world took notice. Suddenly, rap had listeners worldwide, and the rest, as they say, was history.

But before "Rapper's Delight," could be unleashed on the unsuspecting world, somebody had to create the Sugarhill Gang. That credit belongs to Sylvia Robinson. Robinson was a former R&B singer who had started a record label, Sugarhill Records, with her husband. The story is that Sylvia Robinson first heard rap music from her kids. Curious to see if this new sound had potential, she decided to take a chance a produce a rap record. The first rapper she tapped for her new group was Wonder Mike, a buddy of Robinson's oldest son. The second member, Master Gee, auditioned for Robinson when he heard she was putting a group together. Robinson overheard the final member of the group, Big Bank Hank, rhyming and signed him. Apparently, Robinson knew what she was doing in bringing together these three rappers.

"Rapper's Delight" astounded DJs and listeners when it was played on the radio. For DJs unfamiliar with rap, it was a breakthrough. For DJs in the know, it wasn't the fact that rap was being played on the radio that was shocking; rather, the shock had to do with the group that was rapping. No one had heard of the Sugarhill Gang!

The Sugarhill Gang went on to sell millions of copies. At the time, most music industry people believed that rap music was just another trend. Now, more than twenty years later, we know better!

► What changed in rap music once "Rapper's Delight" was released?

A   the Sugarhill Gang split up
B   people lost interest in rap music
C   Sylvia Robinson became a rapper
D   rap gained increased popularity

Now that you're groovin' to the beat, answer the sample question using the **Know It All Approach.** Start by reading the passage carefully. Underline the words that you think are the most interesting and important. Then, carefully read the question and all of the four answer choices.

What do you think about answer choice (A)? The question asks what changed in rap music once "Rapper's Delight" was released. Does the passage mention that the *Sugarhill Gang split up*? Look back at the passage. That information is not noted or inferred. Answer choice (A) is not correct.

What about answer choice (B)? Does the passage infer that *people lost interest in rap music*? Look back at the passage. The passage infers just the opposite: people gained interest because of the release of "Rapper's Delight." Answer choice (B) is not correct.

What about answer choice (C)? Does the passage infer that *Sylvia Robinson became a rapper*? Look back at the passage. That information is not inferred. Answer choice (C) is not correct.

Look at answer choice (D). Does the passage infer that rap *gained increased popularity* once "Rapper's Delight" was released? Look back at the passage. You are told that "Rapper's Delight" was the first rap song to hit the Top 40 charts. You are also told that its wide release made hip-hop instantly international. You can infer that rap music gained increased popularity with the release of "Rapper's Delight." Answer choice (D) is the correct answer.

The **Know It All Approach** has helped you find the correct answer: answer choice (D). The correct answer choice has to be supported by information in the passage. Always use the information in the passage to identify the correct answer.

Get a grip on these passages and questions.

The Life of a Baseball

Ever wonder how the skin of a baseball is sewn on? All those sharp turns, the exact string tension that creates just the right seams—it's easier to imagine a baseball stork giving birth to baseballs than to envision a sewing machine that could manage the job! Actually, there's neither a baseball stork nor a machine that sews the skin on a baseball. Unbelievably, most baseballs are sewn together by hand!

A baseball starts as a small sphere of cork. Then, the cork core is surrounded by a rubber shell. Half of the rubber shell is black. The other half is red. At this stage, a baseball is known as a "pill." The pill grows by being wound with three layers of wool yarn. After the ball has been wrapped in wool, a layer of cotton is wrapped around the ball. This layer of cotton is what makes the ball smooth. The final layer, a cowhide cover, is fixed to the cotton with rubber cement. The cowhide cover is extremely tight-fitting and must be sewn on over this sticky and extremely firm lump.

It is at this stage, the baseball-sewing expert steps up to the plate. The sewing expert uses a device that holds the sticky baseball with the leather cover wrapped around it. The sewer must make 108 stitches in the ball, following stitching holes that have already been punched into the ball. The sewer starts at the narrowest part of the cover, known as the "neck," and stitches down the seam with custom-made needles. The ball is dampened so that it is flexible and the sewer must manipulate the ball and the needle to stitch up the rest of the ball. This is no easy task! The sewer must use a foot-pedal controlled vise to turn the ball around in order to get at any hard to reach sections. Although it's meticulous and time-consuming work, experts generally sew four to six baseballs an hour. After the sewing is complete, it's time for the final stage, during which a wooden press rolls the baseball-to-be's seams flat. In order to protect the balls from humidity, finished balls are stored in a dehumidifying room.

A ruler and a scale put the resulting ball to the test: at this stage, a ball must have a circumference that falls between 9 and 9.25 inches and weigh between 5 and 5.25 ounces. Baseballs that don't measure up are know as "lemons." The lemons are used in batting practice or become stadium gift shop items. The balls that make the grade soon end up on the pitchers mound in a major league game.

1. If weight of the baseball was not between 5 and 5.25 ounces, the most likely result would be

    A   that it is used in batting practice.
    B   that the sewing expert let it pass through.
    C   the sewing experts take it home for their kids.
    D   the ball would have a larger neck.

2. When the balls leave the dehumidifying room where are they likely to go?

    A   back to the baseball-sewing expert
    B   back to the plant to become pills
    C   to stores where people buy them
    D   to the wooden press to be rolled

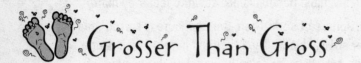

Zit Chat

Zena had a lot of zits when she was a teenager. Now Zena is a dermatologist with beautiful, clear skin who travels to high schools across the nation sharing zit information with teens. Today Zena is giving a lecture in the auditorium at Know It All High School. Listen in!

"We all get them, we all hate them! Trust me, I know all about zits. They're gross, embarrassing, and ugly! When I started high school, it was as if my zits decided to start high school too! All four years, they followed me everywhere—then, miraculously, when it was time for me to graduate, they decided to stay behind. They left me, or I left them, and I am glad to say that we have never had a reunion since!

"So why do zits decide to do high school with some of you? Well, during your teen years your body starts to do some bizarre things, including producing more testosterone. No, testosterone has nothing to do with tests! It's a male hormone that females have too, but in different amounts. Testosterone is responsible for telling your body to produce more oil. Dead skin cells mix with all that oil and clog your pores. All of which results in zits!

"Testosterone, though, is not the only thing that causes zits. Worried about your grades? Scared of upcoming tests? In a fight with your best friend? Stress can cause zits! Stress is not just in your mind; in fact, stress finds its way onto your physical body by claiming territory on your face or body in the form of pimples. Also, if you have an infection of some sort, it may well make an appearance as pimples.

"Any questions from the audience? How about you, raising your hand in the first row. What's your question?"

"Does chocolate cause acne?"

"You're in luck! There were recent tests conducted that found that eating chocolate had no effect on acne."

"You, over there in the blue shirt—what's your question?"

"My friend told me that only dirty people get acne. Is that true?"

"Don't laugh folks! It's a reasonable question. The answer is that bacteria lurks in everyone's skin, whether you're clean or dirty, fourteen or forty-five. Zits don't care about your color or your age or your gender.

"Well, times up, folks. Remember to be good to your skin—it will stay with you the rest of your life. Wash your face every morning and night. Drink eight glasses of water, and eat a balanced diet. And do not pick at your zits unless you want scars! When you see a zit in the mirror, smile at it—in a few days, it will be a thing of the past!"

3. Which of the following will most likely happen next?

   A The students will leave the auditorium and return to their classes.
   B Zena will speak privately to the students that have acne.
   C Zena will escort the students back to their classrooms.
   D The students will perform a skit about zits for Zena before she leaves..

4. Zena's face most likely cleared up because

   A   she washed with special soaps each day.
   B   she stopped eating chocolate.
   C   she smiled at her zits.
   D   she was past adolescence.

5. How did Zena most likely know that dirty people are not the only ones who get acne? Support your answer with information from the passage.

_____

_____

_____

_____

_____

_____

_____

_____

6. In general, who can get zits?

    A everyone

    B teenagers

    C people who love chocolate

    D dirty people

Subject Review

This chapter was full of rap music firsts, baseball trivia, and facts about zits, but it was also full of useful information.

An **inference** requires that you use your reason and experience to come up with an idea, based on what an author implies or suggests. Inferences should be based on supporting details from the text you are reading as well as your own knowledge.

A **conclusion** is a general statement you can make and explain with reasoning, or with supporting details from a text.

A **prediction** is a guess what will happen next. When you predict, you are drawing an inference.

A **generalization** is an inference that can apply to more than one item or group. A generalization has a more general scope than a prediction or a conclusion.

Now you should be able to answer the questions from the beginning of the chapter.

How did Sylvia Robinson know that the Sugarhill Gang would be a successful group?

She didn't know they would be successful. She put the three rappers together and took a chance on them. It was lucky for her and for the rappers that "Rapper's Delight" was so successful.

It's likely that baseball-sewing experts

A have a lot of patience.

B are not detail oriented.

C play pro baseball.

D have sticky hands.

The correct answer is choice (A) have a lot of patience. In order to sew 108 stitching holes, a lot of patience as well as good eyesight are needed!

What changed for Zena once she graduated from high school?

Her face full of zits cleared up and her skin became beautiful and clear.

CHAPTER 7
Genre and Purpose

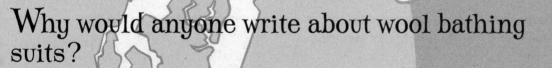

Why would anyone write about wool bathing suits?

Where could you find facts about hypnotism?

Why does a passage about the Cyclone exist?

Bulk up your brain by completing this chapter about genre and purpose. Know It All! fact: "genre" comes from middle French, where it originally meant "gender."

Genre

A **genre** is a category that describes the style and content of a passage. *Know It All!* is a workbook, which is very different from a newspaper, which is very different from a poem, which is very different from many other genres.

Check out this list of genres.

- **Novel:** lengthy work of fiction, often with a complex plot and cast of characters (for example, *Fahrenheit 451* by Ray Bradbury)

- **Short Story:** short work of fiction, often with a specific, simple plot and only a few characters (for example, *The Lottery* by Shirley Jackson)

- **Reference Book:** factual information about a wide variety of subjects (for example, *The Encyclopedia Britannica*)

- **Biography:** factual information about the life of a real person (for example, *Nelson Mandela: A Biography* by Martin Meredith)

- **Play:** usually a work of fiction dramatically performed on a stage (for example, *A Midsummer Night's Dream* by William Shakespeare)

- **Poem:** can be fictional or factual but can be written with line breaks, rhyme, and rhythm, and sometimes without full sentences (for example, *Ode to Salt* by Pablo Neruda)

The Purpose of Text

Texts are written to have many different purposes. Some texts are written to be entertaining, some are written to be informative, and some are written to be persuasive. An author can combine purposes in a single passage and write a text that entertains, informs, and persuades all at the same time.

One of the most common purposes of texts, such as biographies, informative articles, and reference books, is to inform. Other texts, such as short stories, plays, poems, and novels, are supposed to entertain the reader. Finally, some texts, such as editorials in newspapers, advertisements, and persuasive essays, are intended to persuade.

Now, check out this example.

Hip History

When Fifteen Pound Bathing Suits Were All the Rage

In the late 1800s, people traveled to ocean beaches to feel the Sun warm their skin, the breeze tickle their hair, and the sand squish between their feet. But they did not go to swim! Most people would only go so far as dipping their toes into the water. People worried that sea water could remove the salts that naturally occurred in the body. A strange idea when you consider the saltiness of seawater. Nowadays, a swimmer who finds his or her mouth full of ocean water usually exclaims, "Ugh." Back then, someone with a mouth full of ocean water may have thought, "Has the salt in this water been stolen from my toes or the toes of someone in my family? Am I tasting Aunt Margaret's feet?" Swimming in the ocean was a very different experience back then.

As a result of this concern about the "dangers" of salt water, bathers wore thick bathing suits that covered most of their bodies. Doctors recommended that bathing suits be made from wool or thick flannel to protect swimmers. Additionally, specific colors were recommended to help bathers stay healthy. Today, doctors warn bathers against wearing dark colors. We now know that dark colors absorb heat and bathers who spend the day on the beach wearing a dark garment may risk getting overheated. But in the 1870s, blue, maroon, brown, and gray were choice colors for bathing suits. Once one of these dark wool or flannel suits got wet, they could weigh up to fifteen pounds!

Eventually, people risked the salty waters and swimming in the ocean became a popular pastime. That took a few years and a lot of toe-flavored water was swallowed along the way.

▶ Which of the following was most likely the author's purpose for writing the passage?

A   to prove that swimming in the salty water is a health risk
B   to share a story about a swimmer in the late 1800s getting a mouth full of water
C   to compare the effects of wool bathing suits to the effects of flannel bathing suits
D   to inform readers about swimming in the ocean in the late 1800s

Now that your brain is soaked with information, use it to figure out the answer the sample question. Use the **Know It All Approach** to help you out.

Start by reading the passage carefully. Underline the words that you think are the most interesting and important. Then carefully read the question and all of the four answer choices.

What do you think about answer choice (A)? Do you think that the author wrote the passage *to prove that swimming in the salty water is a health risk*? Look back at the passage. The author describes how people once thought swimming in salt water posed a health risk but then calls this a "strange idea." Answer choice (A) is not correct.

What about answer choice (B)? Did the author write the passage *to share a story about a swimmer in the late 1800s getting a mouth full of water*? Look back to the passage. Although the first paragraph makes a joke about this, most of the passage is not about this. Answer choice (B) is not correct.

What about answer choice (C)? Do you think that the author wrote the passage *to compare the effects of wool bathing suits to the effects of flannel bathing suits*? The author mentions that bathing suits were made of wool and flannel, but the author never compares the two. Answer choice (C) is not correct.

What about answer choice (D)? Did the author write the passage *to inform readers about swimming in the ocean in the late 1800s*? The first paragraph describes how people in the late 1800s felt about swimming in the ocean, and the second paragraph describes the types of bathing suits they wore. Therefore, answer choice (D) is correct.

The **Know It All Approach** has helped you find the correct answer: answer choice (D). The correct answer choice has to be supported by information in the passage. You may know information about swimming, but you shouldn't rely on outside information. Always use the information in the passage to identify the correct answer.

Now concentrate on these passages and questions.

You Are Feeling Sleepy

Does hypnosis actually work? Some doctors believe it does. For more than two centuries, doctors around the world have been using hypnosis. Yet after all this time, no one can explain how a hypnotist could make a person believe he or she is a chicken. Although researchers are not sure exactly how hypnosis works, they do know that hypnosis affects the brain. The brain of a person in a hypnotic state shows increased blood flow.

Most modern doctors trained in hypnosis believe that a few things are crucial to having a successful hypnosis session. First, a patient needs to attain an intense concentration to be hypnotized. Second, a patient must be willing and open to the doctor's suggestions. For example, if a doctor said, "You will believe you are a chicken and want to eat worms," and a patient said, "No, I want to believe I am a cow and eat grass!" then the hypnosis will probably not work.

Modern doctors use hypnosis to help people overcome phobias, get rid of bad habits, become better workers, reduce or eliminate pain during operations, and a vast number of other uses. According to these doctors and their patients, hypnosis works.

1. From which of the following was the passage probably taken?
   A   a poem
   B   a biography
   C   a newspaper
   D   a play

2. The main purpose of the passage is
   A   to entertain readers with amusing anecdotes about hypnotizing worms.
   B   to teach readers how to successfully conduct a hypnosis session.
   C   to present readers with factual information about hypnosis and research on hypnosis.
   D   to persuade readers that hypnosis works for all patients all the time and should be used by all doctors.

Riding the Cyclone

There are many things to do on Coney Island. You can watch minor league baseball, enjoy a hot dog on the boardwalk, visit the aquarium, or ride the Ferris wheel. But, for sheer thrills, nothing—and I mean nothing!—beats the Coney Island Cyclone. The Cyclone might be one of the oldest coasters in America, but this classic coaster is still one of the best.

A Scream Back in Time

Around the turn of the twentieth century, the first roller coaster on Coney Island was created. It was a simple ride on which passengers rolled back and forth on a strip of railroad track. As the popularity of Coney Island grew, more and more roller coasters appeared. Coney Island visitors were soon riding the Loop-the-Loop, the Tornado, and the Thunderbolt.

Wheeeeee!!!

In the late 1920s, the Cyclone debuted in Coney Island. It was built to be scarier than the popular Thunderbolt and Tornado, and it succeeded. It starts with an 86-foot drop, before flying around numerous twists and turns. Charles Lindbergh, the pilot who flew the first non-stop trip across the Atlantic Ocean, described a ride on the Cyclone as "greater than flying an airplane at top speed." And in the middle of the 1900s, the Cyclone was given credit for performing a medical wonder. As the tale is told, a man with aphonia, a disease that limited his ability to speak, took a ride. When the ride ended and the roller coaster pulled to a stop, the man said, "I feel sick." Then he fainted, astonished at having just spoken.

Unlike many of the newer metal roller coasters, the Cyclone is made of wood. But this adds to the thrills! For me there's nothing as thrilling as hearing the chink-chink-chink as the train pulls our car and the wood creaks a little just before we drop down and the wind makes my lips buzz. There is nothing like spending a summer riding the Cyclone.

3. The author probably divided the passage into sections in order to

    A   convince readers that wooden roller coasters are boring.
    B   emphasize different types of details.
    C   list each amusement park in the order that it was developed.
    D   amuse readers by providing funny titles to each section.

4. Describe how the words the author chose and the style that the author used to write this passage supported the author's purpose. Support your answer with details from the passage.

    _____

    _____

    _____

    _____

    _____

    _____

    _____

5. From which of the following was the passage "Riding the Cyclone" probably taken?

    A   an informational article
    B   a collection of poetry
    C   an anthology of short stories
    D   a biography

6. Which of the following would **most likely** contain more information about the Cyclone in Coney Island?

    A   *Velocity and Screaming: The Physics of Roller Coasters*
    B   *How to Ride Roller Coasters and Not Barf*
    C   *A Cyclone Summer: A Detective Miller Mystery*
    D   *Let's Ride Again: A History of the Cyclone*

Subject Review

Have you got the knack for identifying genres? Can you spot the purpose of a given passage? This chapter was full of odd ideas and classic coasters, but it was also full of useful information.

Genre is a category that describes the style and content of a passage.

Check out this list of different genres.

Novel: lengthy work of fiction, often with a complex plot and cast of characters

Short Story: short work of fiction, often with a specific, simple plot and only a few characters

Reference Book: factual information about a wide variety of subjects

Biography: factual information about the life of a real person

Play: usually a work of fiction dramatically performed on a stage

Poem: can be fictional or factual but can be written with line breaks, rhyme, and rhythm, and sometimes without full sentences

Texts are written for many different purposes. Some texts **inform,** some **entertain,** and others **persuade.**

Now you should be able to answer the questions from the beginning of the chapter:

Why would anyone write about wool bathing suits?
Because wool swimsuits are going to be all the rage next season. No! Because the author wanted to inform readers about swimming in the oceans at the turn of the twentieth century.

Where could you find facts about hypnotism?
A passage about hypnotism would probably be in a newspaper.

Why does a passage about the Cyclone exist?
Because the author researched about the Cyclone in Coney Island and wrote the information in a passage so that you could **learn** about it!

Run, People, Run!

While running with bulls may sound like an odd way to have fun, each year thousands of adventurous souls travel to Pamplona, Spain, to do just that. The running of the bulls is part of the San Fermin Festival, which takes place between the July 7 and 14 each year. Every morning during this week, six bulls and two herds of tame bulls are set free from their corral. The bulls form a small pack and run through the city streets, making a traditional route to the bullfighting rink.

In front of these bulls thousands of excited thrill seekers run, trying desperately to keep their footing in the ancient cobblestone streets and stay ahead of the bulls.

The run lasts for approximately three minutes; however, if any of the bulls should be separated from its brothers, as they often are, it takes longer. It begins when a skyrocket is launched from the corrals. When the runners see this signal, they know it is time to get the lead out! Runners must be especially careful when the reach the curve of Calle Merdaderes and the area between the Calle Estafeta and the Bull Ring. Bull Run tradition holds that these two areas are the most dangerous stretches of street in the run. The winding streets get narrower at these two points and it can lead to dangerous overcrowding. How dangerous? Between the 1920s and now, the Bull Run has been the cause of more than a dozen deaths and hundreds of injured runners.

If the Bull Run sounds like the newest reality television show, guess again. The San Fermin festival can be traced back to the thirteenth and fourteenth-centuries. The festival still has a religious nature to it as it did in the past; however, over time the festival has come to include other elements such as music, dance, theater, fireworks, fiestas, and bullfights.

The event gained worldwide popularity in the twentieth century, when Ernest Hemingway described it in his novel, *The Sun Also Rises.* After the novel appeared in 1926, Hemingway aficionados from all over the world were inspired to head to Pamplona for the week-long festival. Beware: reading *The Sun Also Rises* may have you packing your bags and heading to the festival. If you should find yourself Pamplona this July, keep these useful tips in mind.

- Wear clothes which are appropriate for the run.

- Do not grab or obstruct the bulls during the run.

- Do no hide in a corner on the course the bulls run.

- Be careful!

1. What is the main idea of the passage?

   A The running of the bulls, a part of the San Fermin Festival, is a dangerous event that many people take part in each year.

   B If you run with bulls, you need to be careful when you reach the curve of Calle Merdaderes and the area between the Calle Estafeta and the Bull Ring.

   C After Hemingway's novel appeared in 1926, people from all over the world were inspired to head to Pamplona for the week-long festival.

   D The San Fermin Festival can be traced back to the thirteenth and fourteenth centuries, when it was a strictly religious event.

2. Which of the following sentences best summarizes the third paragraph?

   A The San Fermin Festival is extremely dangerous.

   B The San Fermin Festival has evolved over time.

   C The San Fermin Festival began in the thirteenth century.

   D The festival still has a religious nature to it.

3. What is the theme if the passage? Use information from the passage to support your answer.

   _____

   _____

   _____

CHAPTER 8
Comparing and Contrasting

How does the "waggle" dance differ from the "tremble" dance?

How was world sailing champion Ellen MacArthur different when she was 10 years old?

How does the Millennium Force roller coaster differ from the Superman Ride of Steel roller coaster?

Finding similarities and differences between concepts is an important skill. Conquer this chapter on comparing and contrasting.

Compare and Contrast

To **compare** is to discuss the similarities between two or more things. For example, tennis and soccer are alike because they are both sports.

To **contrast** is to discuss the differences between two or more things. For example, tennis and soccer are different because one is played on a tennis court and the other is played on a soccer field.

When you compare two ideas, the following transition words can be helpful: *similarly, like*, and *in the same way*. Here's an example of how you would use one of these transition words to make a comparison: "Like Arthur, David was a fiction writer."

When you contrast two ideas, the following transition words and phrases can be helpful: *however, although, in contrast, on the other hand*, and *unlike*. Here's an example of how you would use one of these transition words to contrast two ideas: "Barrie loves dogs, unlike her sister, who prefers cats."

When you are reading, pay special attention to similarities or differences about characters, places, and details the author shares with you. These similarities and differences will often help you to gain insight and better understand an article or story.

Be careful not to misinterpret information you are given. If you are unsure of the author's intent, look back at the passage and try to make sense of the information in the context in which it is appears.

Put on your dancing shoes before you check out this example.

Alternative Animals

Bee Bop

Imagine you communicated not by talking, but by dancing. Maybe you would do a little tap dance to tell your friends you were excited. Perhaps you would perform a quick box step to tell your parents that you were going out. As strange as this seems, there is at least one place you can find an animal that communicates through dance. Just find a honeybee and follow it to her hive. (If you catch a honeybee working, you can be sure it is female because the males, or drones, don't work.) Then, watch the honeybee bust a move on her special dance floor located near the entrance of the hive. She will dance a figure-eight pattern and flutters her wings.

What's the bee bop all about? Actually, the "waggle" dance is a form of communication that serves bees the way speech serves humans. When a bee wants to let other bees in on a nectar source that has been discovered, the bee performs the "waggle" dance. The reason that the dance floor is located near the entrance of the hive is so that foragers (bees that store nectar) can quickly be on their way to the nectar source after watching and learning from the dance. The dance floor is the equivalent to a conference room for bees. When a bee arrives back at the nest with news to share, the bee goes right to the dance floor. Other bees gather around and wait for the news.

During the "waggle" dance, the bee communicates important pieces of information. For instance, the longer she "waggles," the farther the source of nectar is from the hive. The dancing bee shares with the group how rich the source is by how long or how vigorously she dances. She indicates the direction of the nectar source by her walk in the waggle dance. In addition, the boogying bee shares the odor of the flowers in question with the other bees, which get a whiff with their antennae.

Two other dances that honeybees perform are the "shake" dance and the "tremble" dance. When nectar sources are so rich that more foragers are needed, a worker bee performs the "shake" dance. During the "shake" dance the worker bee shakes her abdomen back and forth before a forager who she wants to get to work. When more bees are needed to process the nectar that forager bees have brought back to the hive, a worker bee performs the "tremble" dance. During the "tremble" dance the bee walks slowly around the nest, causing her body to tremble by quivering her legs. During the "tremble" dance, the bee looks all shook up.

▶ According to the passage, a honeybee's dance can best be compared to

A   the newest dance craze
B   a dance marathon
C   a figure-eight pattern
D   a human's use of speech

Now that you heard the latest buzz, figure out the answer to the sample question using the **Know It All Approach.**

Start by reading the passage carefully. Underline the words that you think are the most interesting and important. Then carefully read the question and all of the four answer choices.

What do you think about answer choice (A)? Does the passage compare a honeybee's dance to *the newest dance craze*? Look back at the passage. It mentions dancing in the first sentence, but are the honeybee dances ever compared to the newest dance crazes? Look at each of the other choices to see if there's a better answer before you make a final decision.

What about answer choice (B)? Does the passage mention that a honeybee's dance is similar to *a dance marathon*? Look back at the passage. It makes no mention of dance marathons. Answer choice (B) is not correct.

What about answer choice (C)? Does the passage compare a honeybee's dance to *a figure-eight pattern*? Look back at the passage. A figure-eight pattern is part of the "waggle" dance, but no comparisons are formed regarding it. Answer choice (C) is not correct.

Look at answer choice (D). Does the passage compare a honeybee's dance to *a human's use of speech*? Look back at the passage. It states that "the waggle dance is a form of communication that serves bees the way speech serves humans." Therefore, answer choice (D) is correct.

The **Know It All Approach** has helped you find the correct answer: answer choice (D). The correct answer choice has to be supported by information in the passage. Always use the information in the passage to identify the correct answer. Be sure to read each of the answer choices before you make a final decision.

Now sail on with these passages and questions.

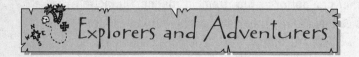

Going Places

    In 2002, twenty-four-year-old Ellen MacArthur sailed around the world alone in 94 days, 4 hours, 25 minutes, and 40 seconds. That single achievement scored her two major records. She became the woman with the fastest time circumnavigating the globe and the youngest sailor to circle the world solo in a nonstop race! That's no small feat, considering that MacArthur was the youngest, smallest, and only female competitor in the Vendee Globe, a brutal 25,000-mile boat race. Although she came in second place (the winner was a French sailor finished one day earlier), she fulfilled a lifelong dream by finishing the grueling race.

MacArthur wasn't always in the top ranks. In fact, when she was ten, she finished last place in all the races at a sailing school. Unlike the other young sailors, MacArthur's boat and equipment was not top-quality. After coming in last, MacArthur made a promise to herself that she would never come in last again. She refused to be last, no matter how hard the race.

Apparently, MacArthur is keeping this promise. In 2003, she went to sea on another attempt to break the record for sailing non-stop around the world. Unfortunately, she encountered unforeseen hardships during this expedition—her boat lost its mast!—but she has not given up her sailing dreams. She has a lot of sailing adventures in her future. While many people daydream about following their passions and being adventurous, MacArthur turned her daydreams into realities. Like other courageous adventurers, MacArthur understands that there will be difficult days. "You deal with it," she says. "That's what makes the experience richer."

1. How was MacArthur's sailing race in 2002 different from the sailing races she competed in when she was ten years old?

   A   She didn't come in last place.
   B   Her equipment was worse.
   C   It made her stop racing.
   D   She was always daydreaming.

2. The author compares MacArthur to

   A   all the sailors who raced before her.
   B   the man who won the race in 2002.
   C   other courageous adventurers.
   D   a woman who comes in last place.

For Your Amusement

Hold on!

Roxy, the roller coaster fanatic, is on a mission to uncover the craziest, coolest roller coasters. Roxy loves when people join her on her adventures: "It's no fun to travel alone!" she says. "Besides, I get scared when I am cruising alone at top speeds loop-de-looping. Come along for the adventure!"

First stop is the *Millennium Force* in Ohio. According to Roxy, this is the first coaster to break the 300-foot height barrier. It travels at a skin plastering 93 miles per hour! Just as Roxy gets on line, she remembers that she has to make a phone call. "Hey, why don't you go for a ride and tell me how it was?" Roxy says. "Have fun!" Then, poof, she's gone. The ticket taker is asking for your ticket and you are being strapped in tight. Have fun is what you think as the ride begins.

"Me, scared of roller coasters?" Roxy says when you next meet up. "Not a chance! I'm all about adventure. When I was 12 years old, I was too short to ride the coasters. I made a promise to myself that as soon as I was tall enough I would travel the world riding every coaster there was!"

Next stop is the *Superman Ride of Steel* in Massachusetts. Roxy has uncovered the facts on this mean steel machine that is more than 200 feet tall. It's full of hills and outrageous twists and turns. The first drop is 221 feet! "That's almost 45 times my height," says Roxy, who is barely five feet tall. "Is today Tuesday?" Roxy says as she waits on line. She does a little trance dance flailing her arms and shaking her head. "Tuesday is the day I wash my hair. I have to go, now! But why don't you stay? It's almost our turn to board. I expect to hear all about the ride! Be sure to hold on tight! Have fun, buh bye!" You have a strange feeling of having been there before. Have fun you think and the coaster is taking you awayyyyyyyyyy.

Roxy is proud of her collection of tickets to ride. Her hair all clean and shiny, and she shows you her collection. "Here's one from the *Magnum XL-200* in Ohio. It has a lift hill that rises all the way to 205 feet!" says Roxy. "This one over here is from *Montu* in Busch Gardens, Florida. It's an inverted coaster that has trains that hang underneath the rails so that when you ride it your legs float free, ski-lift style."

You can still feel your stomach dropping although it's been a day since you were on the *Superman Ride of Steel*. You know that if Roxy had actually ridden those coasters, she would have had to give her tickets to the ticket holders. When you ask why she still has the tickets to ride, she says, "Yikes! I just realized that I didn't feed my cat! Gotta go—see ya around!"

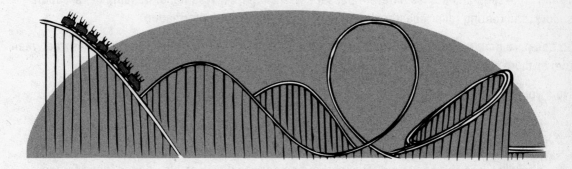

3. What is the difference between the *Millennium Force* and the *Superman Ride of Steel?*

    A   The *Millennium Force* is 300 feet tall while the *Superman Ride of Steel* is 200 feet tall.
    B   The *Millennium Force* is made of steel while the *Superman Ride of Steel* is not made of steel.
    C   The *Superman Ride of Steel* is more fun than the *Millennium Force.*
    D   The *Superman Ride of Steel* is less expensive to ride than the *Millennium Force.*

4. What does Roxy compare to the drop of the 221-foot drop of the Superman *Ride of Steel?*

    A   her hair
    B   her height
    C   her weight
    D   her age

5. Look back to the previous passage about Ellen MacArthur. How did Ellen MacArthur's courageous spirit differ from Roxy's courageous spirit? Use information from both passages to support your answer.

    _____

    _____

    _____

    _____

    _____

Subject Review

Are you a compare and contrast expert? Do you know how to find the similarities and differences within a passage and across different passages? This chapter was full of dancing bees, superb sailors, and roaring roller coasters, but it was also full of useful information.

To compare things is to discuss their similarities. To contrast is to discuss the differences between two or more things.

Now you should be able to answer the questions from the beginning of the chapter:

How does the "waggle" dance differ from the "tremble" dance?

The worker bee dances the "waggle" dance when she wants to inform other bees of a nectar source she has found. The worker bee dances the "tremble" dance when foragers have brought so much nectar back to the hive that more bees are needed to process the nectar into honey.

How was world sailing champion Ellen MacArthur different when she was ten years old?

When she was ten years old, Ellen MacArthur came in last place in all the races at sailing school.

How does the Millennium Force roller coaster differ from the Superman Ride of Steel roller coaster?

The Millennium Force breaks the 300-feet height barrier while the Superman Ride of Steel is shorter at more than 200 feet tall.

CHAPTER 9
Poetry

"That music hath a far more pleasing sound"

"My mistress, when she walk, treads on the ground"

Sound and ground are examples of what poetry technique?

What secret message did Edgar Allan Poe hide in his poem The Enigma?

Read these lines of poetry from Grace Hazard Conkling's The Little Rose is Dust, My Dear.

The little rose is dust, my dear;

The elfin wind is gone

That sang a song of silver words

And cooled our hearts with dawn.

Name two poetic techniques that appear in these lines.

Muses, in Greek mythology, were goddesses who inspired artists. Get ready to mean the muses by completing this chapter about poetry.

Poetry

Poetry can be fictional or factual and can be written with line breaks, rhyme, and rhythm, and sometimes without full sentences.

Poetry can incorporate any or all of the following techniques:

Alliteration: Alliteration is the repetition of sounds, most often consonant sounds, at the beginnings of words. For example, Apples always attack me in autumn when I sit under the apple tree.

Meter: Meter is a regular pattern of stressed and unstressed syllables that gives a line of poetry a predictable rhythm. The unit of meter within a line is called a foot. Each type of foot has a unique pattern of stressed and unstressed syllables.

Rhyme: Rhyme is the repetition of the same stressed vowel sounds and any succeeding sounds in two or more words. *End rhymes* occur at the ends of lines of poetry. Rhyme that occurs within a single line is called *internal rhyme*. *Slant rhymes* occur when words include sounds that are similar but do not rhyme exactly.

Free verse: Free verse is poetry that has no fixed pattern of meter and rhyme. Free verse often uses sound devices and a rhythm similar to that of human speech.

Imagery: Imagery is the word pictures that writers create to help evoke an emotional response. To create effective images, writers use *sensory details*, or descriptions that appeal to one or more of the five sense; sight, hearing, touch, taste, and smell.

Onomatopoeia: Onomatopoeia is the use of a word or phrase that imitates or suggests the sound of what it describes. Some examples are buzz, whoosh, shush, and swish.

Stanza: A stanza is a group of lines forming a unit in a poem.

Now dig into a little poetry yourself. Check out the following poem and see if you can answer the sample question.

 Hip History

Poetic Freedom

In his poem, *Song of Myself*, written in the nineteenth century, Walt Whitman uses free verse as a tool to express his thoughts, ideas, beliefs, and emotions. Free verse allows him to speak to his readers in a way that is free of rules and restrictions. At the time it was published, this poem was controversial because Whitman not only strayed from contemporary conventions in poetry, but he showed man as a part of the natural world in a new and invigorating way.

Here is an excerpt from *Song of Myself*:

I believe a leaf of grass is no less than the journeywork of the stars,
And the pismire is equally perfect, and a grain of sand, and the egg
    of the wren,
And the tree toad is a chef-d'oeuvre for the highest,
And the running blackberry would adorn the parlors of heaven,
And the narrowest hinge in my hand puts to scorn all the machinery,
And the cow crunching with depressed head surpasses any statue,
And a mouse is a miracle enough to stagger sextillions of infidels,
And I could come every afternoon of my life to look at the farmer's
    Girl boiling her iron teakettle and baking shortcake.

▶ "Cow crunching" is an example of which of the following?

A free verse
B stanza
C alliteration
D meter

Now that you have gained your poetic independence, figure out the answer to the sample question.

Start by reading the passage carefully. Underline the words that you think are the most interesting and important. Then carefully read the question and all of the four answer choices.

What do you think about answer choice (A)? Is "cow crunching" an example of *free verse*? It's part of a sentence that's free verse, but on its own, it is not free verse. Answer choice (A) is not correct.

What about answer choice (B)? Is "cow crunching" an example of a *stanza*? A stanza consists of a group of lines that form a unit in a poem. Answer choice (B) is not correct.

What about answer choice (C)? Is "cow crunching" an example of *alliteration*? Alliteration is the repetition of sounds, most often consonant sounds, at the beginnings of words. "Cow crunching" fits that description. Read answer choice (D) before you make a decision.

Look at answer choice (D). Is "cow crunching" an example of *meter*? Meter is a regular pattern of stressed and unstressed syllables that gives a line of poetry a predictable rhythm. "Cow crunching" does not fit that description. Answer choice (D) is not correct.

This leaves answer choice (C), which must be the correct answer.

The **Know It All Approach** has helped you find the correct answer: answer choice (C).

There are a couple of things to remember when your answer questions that involve poetry. In a poem, words often take on more meaning because there are usually fewer words in a poem than in a story or passage. Be sensitive to words that might have more than one meaning depending on their context.

When you read a poem, be sure to read it word by word and line by line. Poems are not meant to be skimmed and rushing though a poem is a good way to miss something. Go back and reread lines if something is not clear to you. If possible, read the poem aloud. Sometimes hearing the words helps you to see the images clearer.

Now take some time to read the rhyme and questions below.

Weird Adoration

Sonnet 130 by Shakespeare is a parody, or spoof, of the conventional love poem of Shakespeare's time. In this poem, Shakespeare deliberately makes fun of exaggerated comparisons by suggesting that his lover is ordinary; for example, Shakespeare claims that *I love to hear her speak, yet well I know/ That music hath a far more pleasing sound*. Not a very complimentary thing to say to someone you love! Check out the sonnet and judge for yourself!

Sonnet 130
My mistress' eyes are nothing like the sun;
Coral is far more red than her lips' red:
If snow be white, why then her breasts are dun;
If hairs be wires, black wires grow on her head.
I have seen roses damask'd, red and white,

I love to hear her speak, yet well I know
That music hath a far more pleasing sound:
I grant I never saw a goddess go,—
My mistress, when she walk, treads on the ground:
And yet, by heaven, I think my love as rare
As any she belied with false compare.

1. Look at the following excerpt from the sonnet: *If hairs be wires, black wires grow on her head.* It is an example of which of the following techniques?

    A free verse

    B imagery

    C onomatopoeia

    D rhyme

2. Look at the following excerpts from the sonnet: *My mistress' eyes are nothing like the sun* and *If snow be white, why then her breasts are dun*. Which of the following is true about these lines?

    A they contain an end rhyme   C they are both free verse

    B they do not have a meter   D they use onomatopoeia

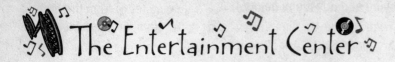

Poe's Enigma

Poet and author Edgar Allan Poe is famous worldwide for his haunting and horrifying tales of terror. What is less known about Poe is his fondness for jokes and riddles. Along side his horror stories, he also wrote humorous tales and detective fiction. In one poem, he combined his interests in puzzles and jokes and created a silly poem that happens to contain a secret message. He dedicated his poem, *The Enigma*, to a friend of his and he hid her name within the poem itself. Take a few minutes to read through the poem below. Don't worry if some of the stranger words are unfamiliar. See if you can crack the code and spell out the hidden name. You get this one hint — the first letter of her name is also the first letter of the first line of the poem: "S."

The Enigma

by Edgar Allan Poe

"Seldom we find," says Solomon Don Dunce,
    "Half an idea in the profoundest sonnet.
Through all the flimsy things we see at once
    As easily as through a Naples bonnet –
Trash of all trash! – how *can* a lady don it?
Yet, heavier far than your Petrarchan stuff –
Owl-downy nonsense that the faintest puff
Twirls into trunk-paper the while you con it."
    And, veritably, Sol is right enough.
The general tuckermanities are arrant
Bubbles – ephemeral and *so* transparent –
But *this* is, now, – you may depend upon it –
Stable, opaque, immortal – all by dint
Of the dear names that lie concealed within't.

Did you find the hidden name? Here's how you break the code. Take the first letter from the first line. Then, take the second letter from the second line and the third letter from the third line. Follow this pattern and you find the hidden name: Sarah Anna Lewis.

3. *"Don Dunce"* is an example of which of the following?

    A   free verse
    B   alliteration
    C   rhyme
    D   onomatopoeia

4. To which of the following does Poe *not* compare the average sonnet?

    A   Solomon Don Dunce
    B   bubbles
    C   a bonnet
    D   trash

5. In the poem, Poe states why he thinks his poem is "immortal." Why does Poe think his poem will be immortal?

    _____

    _____

    _____

    _____

    _____

6. Edgar Allan Poe once used the term "tintinnabulation" to describe to ringing of bells. Of what poetic device is this term an example?

    A   stanza
    B   rhyme
    C   onomatopoeia
    D   free verse

Subject Review

Have you mastered the art of poetry? Are you ready to be a poet and know it? This chapter was full of freedom, compliments, and secrets, but it was also full of useful information. Take a moment to review what you just learned.

Poetry can be fictional or factual and can be written with line breaks, rhyme, and rhythm, and sometimes without full sentences.

Poetry can incorporate any or all of the following techniques:

Alliteration is the repetition of sounds, most often consonant sounds, at the beginnings of words.

Meter is a regular pattern of stressed and unstressed syllables that gives a poem rhythm.

Rhyme is the repetition of the same stressed vowel sounds and any succeeding sounds in two or more words.

Free verse is poetry that has no fixed pattern of meter and rhyme.

Imagery is used by writers to help evoke an emotional response.

Onomatopoeia is the use of a word that imitates the sound of what it describes.

Stanza is a group of lines forming a unit in a poem.

Now you should be able to answer the questions from the beginning of the chapter.

"That music hath a far more pleasing sound"

"My mistress, when she walk, treads on the ground"

Sound and ground are examples of what poetry technique?
Sound and ground rhyme.

What secret message did Edgar Allan Poe hide in his poem The Enigma?
He hid the name of his friend, Sarah Anna Lewis, within the poem.

Read the lines from Grace Hazard Conkling's The Little Rose is Dust, My Dear.

The little rose is dust, my dear;

The elfin wind is gone

That sang a song of silver words

And cooled our hearts with dawn.

Name two poetic techniques that appear in these lines.
There are many techniques used in these lines. Two of the easiest to spot are rhyme and alliteration.

CHAPTER 10
Literary Techniques

How many permanent residents do planners think will live on the Freedom Ship?

What is the slowest animal in the world?

What is slam poetry?

Figure out figures of speech and other writing techniques by mastering this chapter about literary techniques.

Literary Techniques

Literary techniques are tools that authors employ to create vibrant and interesting stories, poems, and plays. There are number of techniques an author can use is staggering, but you don't have to know them all. You should know a handful of the most common tricks an author might use. The first is figurative language. **Figurative language** is language or an expression that is not literally true but expresses some truth beyond the literal level. Figurative language appears in all kinds of writing, but it is especially prominent in poetry. Types of figurative language, also called figures of speech, include the following:

- **Metaphor:** a figure of speech that compares two or more things that have something in common. In contrast to a simile, a metaphor does not use the words *like* or *as*; a metaphor implies the comparison instead of stating it directly.

- **Simile:** a figure of speech using *like* or *as* to compare seemingly unlike things.

- **Personification:** a figure of speech in which an animal, object, force of nature, or idea is given human qualities or characteristics.

Another common technique is the use of allusion. **Allusion** is a reference in a work of literature to a character, place, or situation from history or from another work of literature, music, or art.

Many authors prefer to let their characters do the talking and convey information through the use of dialogue. **Dialogue** is the technical term for written conversation between characters in a literary work.

Sometimes, when an author wants to give you the background to a story, he or she will use a flashback. A **flashback** is an account of an event that happened before a story began. A flashback interrupts the chronological sequence of story events, but gives readers information that may help explain the main events of the story.

Another literary technique is the use of irony. **Irony** is a contrast or discrepancy between appearance and reality or between what is expected and what actually happens. Irony is often hard to spot, because it gets confused with coincidence or just plain old dumb luck. The trick to irony is that there should be a contradiction between the expected and the actual. For example, if a person who is afraid of heights finds themselves on an airplane, that isn't ironic. That's just bad luck. On the other hand, an airplane pilot who is afraid of heights is ironic. There is an unexpected contradiction between being an airline pilot and being afraid of heights.

Know It All! High School Reading

Often writers manipulate the mood of a text. **Mood** is the emotional quality or atmosphere of a story. Writers can control the mood of a story by carefully picking the words the use and the images they choose to focus on.

Use of symbolism is another common technique. **Symbolism** is the use of images to represent internal realities. That sounds complex, but you see it used all the time. People use the American flag, for example, to symbolize patriotism. Symbolism takes something abstract and intangible, like love or anger, and gives the reader a visual sign for it.

Another important technique is the use of tone. **Tone** is the writer or speaker's attitude toward a subject. A writer's tone may convey a variety of attitudes, including sympathy, objectivity, seriousness, sadness, bitterness, or humor. To help find the tone of a story, think about the words that the narrator uses to tell the story. Are the words dull or exciting? Are they positive or negative? You will be able to figure out an author's tone by the words used.

Tips for Answering Literary Technique Questions

The tone of a story can usually be described in more than one way. When you describe the tone of a passage for an open-response question, it's important to support your description with evidence from the passage.

Be careful not to misinterpret the author's tone. If you do, you often lose the message that the author is trying to convey. By reading carefully and paying attention to details, the tone of a story or article becomes evident.

When answering questions about tone be sure to consider the entire passage unless you are asked to do otherwise. If you focus on one event in the story, it is likely that you will not present a complete picture of the tone of the passage.

When answering a question regarding figurative language, be sure to look back at the passage for context clues. The context of figurative language will help you to uncover its meaning and tone. Never assume you know an answer without checking the passage from which it came.

Strap on your life jacket and check out this example.

The Floating City

   In the late 1871, science fiction author Jules Verne wrote a book about an ocean ship so large that people lived on it permanently. They lived, worked, and relaxed all on the confines of this sea-going city. He called his book "The Floating City." Today, more than a century later, a group of engineers, financiers, and dreamers are trying to turn Verne's fantastic vision into reality.

   The twenty-first-century floating city is called the Freedom Ship. First dreamed up by American engineer Norm Nixon in 1994, the plans for this ship steadily grew until, in 1996, the Freedom Ship's planners came up with the current design. As currently envisioned, the Freedom Ship is almost a mile long, 750 feet wide, and more than 25 stories tall. If built, the Freedom Ship would be five times the size of the largest aircraft carrier in the United States Navy.

   The Freedom Ship will be too large to ever dock at any port, but the hope is that the ship and its 60,000 permanent residents will never need to dock. The Freedom Ship will have a small airfield for planes and helicopters on the top deck. The city on the sea will also be wired to land by phone, radio, and Internet connections.

   Why worry about land when everything you need is onboard? The Freedom Ship will, if everything goes according to plan, be able to generate its own power and grow its own food. Its plans include nightclubs, schools, apartments, parks, shopping malls, and anything else a modern city dweller could want.

   So where do you sign up? Not so fast. The Freedom Ship is currently in planning stages and, with a hefty $11 billion price tag, many people wonder if the Freedom Ship will ever be built. Critics charge that the Freedom Ship, at best, is an impossible dream. Others voice concerns about safety issues. Despite these concerns, a small group of underfunded volunteers continue to plan the Freedom Ship.

   Is the Freedom Ship, like the mermaid, just another nautical myth? Or will giant ship someday crisscross the trackless ocean? Only time will tell.

▶ What is the tone of the passage?

A sadness
B excitement
C angry
D caution

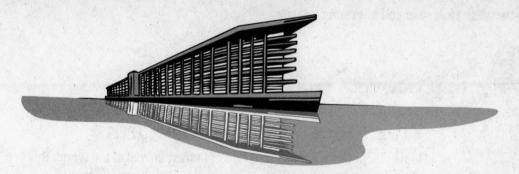

Now try to answer the sample question using the **Know It All Approach.**

Start by reading the passage carefully. Underline the words that you think are the most interesting and important. Then carefully read the question and all of the four answer choices.

What do you think about answer choice (A)? Is the tone of the passage one of *sadness*? Look back to the passage. There is no evidence of that the author is sad about the Freedom Ship. Answer choice (A) is not correct.

What about answer choice (B)? Does the author seem *excited* about the Freedom Ship. What would indicate that the author was excited? The author would state how much they love the idea or the author might use energetic language and exclamation points. Look back at the passage. There is no evidence the author is excited. Answer choice (B) is not correct.

What about answer choice (C)? Is the author *angry*? The author doesn't use any language that would suggest he or she is angry about the Freedom Ship or angry at the people designing it. Answer choice (C) is not the correct answer.

Look at answer choice (D). Would you say the author was *cautious*? The author mentions many of the exciting features of the Freedom Ship, but they also mention what the critics say about the ship. Furthermore, the author is unwilling to say whether or not they think the ship will ever be built. Answer choice (D) is the best answer.

The **Know It All Approach** has helped you find the correct answer: answer choice (D). The correct answer choice has to be supported by information in the passage. Always use the information in the passage to identify the correct answer.

Now try these passages and questions.

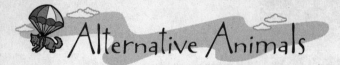

The Slowest Animal on Earth

Many animals compete for the coveted title of fastest animal in the world. But, when it comes to going slow, few animals can compete with the sloth. In the kingdom of lazy animals, the sloth slowly takes the cake.

The sloth is one of the oldest mammals on the planet. A historically inclined sloth could be able to trace its ancestors back to the Late Eocene, about 350 millions years ago. Back then there were five different species of sloth, including the monstrous Megatherium. Imagine a mountain of fur, armor plates, and claws. If anybody had a problem with how slow this elephant-sized sloth moved, they kept it to themselves.

The modern sloth is considerably smaller, measuring only a meter long. From the original five species, only two types of sloth remain: the two-toed sloth and the three-toed sloth. Both live in the jungles of South America.

So, just how slow is the sloth? The name says it all. Nothing rushes these cautious creatures as they slowly move about the jungle, carefully hanging from the limbs of trees. They will cover just a few feet and hour. In fact, sloths move so slowly that moss can actually grow on their fur. Sloths don't mind this green waistcoat; they depend on it. The moss acts as camouflage and helps the sloth stay hidden in their arboreal homes. Because sloths are so slow, hiding is their only real protection against predators.

1. The green waistcoat mentioned in the last paragraph is a metaphor for

    A   the leafy diet of the sloth.
    B   the moss that grows on a sloth's fur.
    C   the jungle home of the sloth.
    D   the fur color of the Megatherium.

2. Which of the following words best describes the tone of the passage?

    A   suspenseful
    B   scientific
    C   mysterious
    D   informal

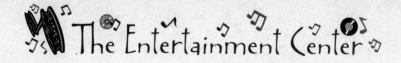

The Entertainment Center

Slamming

Jessica Peters is a slam poet. "Poetry slam is like being on *Star Search*, only everyone is a poet. You stand up in front of the audience and start rhyming and then you get rated for your performance," Jessica says. "It started in the mid-1980s, when I was born. I remember the first time I heard it. My mom took me to a poetry slam down at the community center. I was only five or six years old, but after I heard the audience cheering the poet on and I saw how passionate the poet was, and how the judges sat on the edge of their seats, I knew that I was going to be slamming one day!

"Slam is like swimming to me. I dive in. I get so caught up in the moment and with the audience cheering me on, I look at the microphone and I feel as if we are a team telling a tale.

"There are some rules about poetry slams that you need to know if you want to get started. First, if you want to participate in a slam at a club or community center, you need to sign up with the event's host. The host is the person that finds five audience members to serve as judges. Your poems must be original poems, and you're not allowed to use props, costumes, or musical instruments. There's a time limit to your poems too. If you go over the time limit, points are deducted from your score. If you practice your poems, you should be all set and ready the day of the slam."

Jessica has performed in five slams so far. "In the first round, each poet reads one poem. The top-scoring poets go on to the second round. When you are on stage, it's important to establish a connection with the audience. Make eye contact! The audience is your support when you are up there and the judges are watching you, listening to your every word."

3. Which of the following excerpts is an example of simile?

A *The top-scoring poets go on to the second round*
B *The audience is your support …*
C *Slamming is like swimming to me.*
D *I saw how passionate the poet was …*

4. The words *cheering, passionate, edge of their seats* suggest a mood of

A excitement
B impatience
C indifference
D confusion

Subject Review

Do you *know it all* about literary techniques? This chapter was full of sea adventures, tired animals, and slamming poets, but it was also full of useful information.

Figurative language is language or expressions that are not literally true but express some truth beyond the literal level. Figurative language appears in all kinds of writing, but it is especially prominent in poetry. Types of figurative language called figures of speech include the following:

Allusion is a reference in a work of literature to a character, place, or situation from history or from another work of literature, music, or art.

Dialogue is written conversation between characters in a literary work.

Flashback is an account of an event that happened before a story began.

Irony is a contrast or discrepancy between appearance and reality, or between what is expected and what actually happens.

Mood is the emotional quality or atmosphere of a story.

Symbolism is the use of images to represent internal realities.

Tone is the writer or speaker's attitude toward a subject.

Now you should be able to answer the questions from the beginning of the chapter.

How many permanent residents do planners think will live on the Freedom Ship?
Planners think 60,000 people will live full-time on the Freedom Ship.

What is the slowest animal in the world?
Hands down, the sloth wins that title.

What is slam poetry?
It is competitive poetry reading.

Hip History

Party at the White House

Long ago, I went to a White House inauguration party,
Good thing I was on time and didn't arrive too tardy.
I wouldn't have wanted to miss all the welcome to the White House fun—
Who knew if Andrew Jackson would once again run?

February 1829 was the memorable inauguration date,
That Andrew Jackson threw a party that was first rate.
Washington, D.C., was packed with Andrew Jackson fans,
Wow, becoming president is certainly full of its demands!
When good old Jackson took an oath to rule the nation,
The crowds could all feel the let's party and celebrate vibration.

Compared to other presidential inaugurations his was a rather wild event,
It was a night in which lots of pre-established stuffy president rules were bent.
Partygoers included the highest members of the American political elite,
The crowd became so rowdy that Jackson was forced to slip away, which was
no small feat.
As the party was moved outside, ice cream and wine were the menu,
Adding to the refreshing democratic venue.
Jackson's reign installed a new system of rule—
It certainly didn't hurt that the new prez was cool!

1. According to the passage, compared to other presidential inaugurations, Andrew Jackson's inauguration party was

   A   a new system of rule.
   B   full of its demands.
   C   a rather wild event.
   D   American political elite.

2. "Welcome to the White House" is an example of which of the following?

   A   alliteration
   B   meter
   C   imagery
   D   onomatopoeia

3. Which of the following excerpts from the poem best shows the mood of the poem?

   A   *Wow, becoming president is certainly full of its demands!*
   B   *When good old Jackson took an oath to rule the nation.*
   C   *Who knew if Andrew Jackson would once again run?*
   D   *That Andrew Jackson threw a party that was first rate.*

4. The words *wild, cool, vibration* suggest a mood of

   A   excitement.
   B   boredom.
   C   tiredness.
   D   devotion.

5. What is the tone at the end of the poem?

   A   indifferent
   B   enthusiastic
   C   depressed
   D   faithful

CHAPTER 11
Figurative Language

"Plunging down into the Cave of the Swallows is like dropping down into an underground planet" is an example of _____.

"Foot odor is enough to make a pair of sneakers want to run away" is an example of _____.

"Twins Day Festival is a seeing double event" is an example of _____.

Let your brain bloom like a flower and become sharp as a tack by completing this chapter about figurative language.

Figurative Language

Figurative language is language or an expression that is not literally true but express some truth beyond the literal level. Figurative language appears in all kinds of writing, but it is especially prominent in poetry.

Types of figurative language include the following figures of speech:

- **Metaphor:** A metaphor compares two or more things that have something in common. In contrast to a simile, a metaphor does not use the words *like* or *as*; a metaphor implies the comparison instead of stating it directly. For example, *The sky is an ocean of stars.*

- **Simile:** A simile uses *like* or *as* to compare seemingly unlike things. For example, *Her laughter is like rain that trickles out of her.*

- **Personification:** In personification an animal, object, force of nature, or idea is given human qualities or characteristics. For example, *His breath smelled so horrid that he feared that his toothbrush would run away from him.*

- Never assume you know the answer to a figurative language question without checking the selection. Using context clues, you can make sure you choose the correct answer.

- Figurative language questions usually ask you what the author means by saying certain words. With stories, poems, and articles, you will need to pay attention to the image and meaning of the words.

- Remember to take your time when answering open-response questions about figurative language. Read the question carefully and make sure that you answer every part of it. Use details from the passage to support your answer. Double-check your work afterward.

Dive in by checking out this example.

Mad Science

Plunging

Each year, Andrew and Carl trek seven hours from Mexico City to one of the most bizarre caves in the world: the Cave of the Swallows. It's an abyss that is deep enough to hold the Empire State Building. The cave is named after the tens of thousands of swallows that circle inside its empty chamber.

"The swallows freak Andrew out," Carl says.

"It's not that I am afraid of the swallows—they're just birds that have a short bill, long pointed wings, and often a deeply forked tail," says Andrew. "But when you are coasting way down to the base of the case in the blackness, the swallows look like ghosts coming at you. It's pretty spooky."

"But nothing can keep us from taking that plunge," says Carl. "It's as if you are diving into the deepest part of the ocean. Once you are all strapped in with your parachute and jump, wow! You are flying."

"Sometimes just when I am about to plunge, I imagine my parachute jumping off my back and running away from me, but that's just my fear kicking in. As soon as I jump, I am loving it! You float through the air," says Andrew.

"We spelunkers—that's the term for people like Andrew and me who make a hobby of exploring and studying caves—prefer the thrill of reaching the bottom by parachute, although some folks say that we are risking life and limb by using a parachute."

"The cave's walls sharp and pointy. If we get too close to them, our parachutes could be shredded," Andrew says.

"Our shoots could collapse if one hundred thousand birds gets tangled in our parachutes' lines," Carl adds.

Andrew and Carl look at each other and laugh. They are like two little kids discussing why they love candy even though they know it can give them cavities.

"The journey to the bottom is totally worthwhile," Andrew says.

"Ditto," Carl says. "The scenery at the bottom of the cave is like that of another planet. There's no direct sunlight down there. The walls and floors are covered with shiny green moss. It's totally awesome!" Carl says.

"Awesome," Andrew agrees. "It's a dive into a black hole."

"Only we come back, so it's not really like a black hole," Carl says.

"As much as I love being down there, I am always relieved when it's time to return to the surface," Andrew says.

"Yeah, me too," says Carl. "When that cable comes down to haul us up, and we reach the surface and breathe in the fresh air, I feel as if I have been away from sunlight for days. Plunging is fun, but coming back up is pretty great too!" says Carl.

▶ Which excerpt uses personification, the literary device that describes an object, animal, or idea using human characteristics?

A *They are like two little kids discussing why they love candy.*
B *The landscape at the base of the cave is like that of another planet.*
C *I imagine my parachute jumping off my back and running away from me . . .*
D *I feel as if I have been away from sunlight for days.*

Now come up for air and figure out the answer to the sample question using the **Know It All Approach.** Start by reading the passage carefully. Underline the words that you think are the most interesting and important. Then, carefully read the question and all of the four answer choices.

What do you think about answer choice (A)? Does this excerpt describe an object, animal, or idea using human characteristics? No. But this choice does contain a simile—it uses the word "like" to compare two things. Answer choice (A) is not correct.

What about answer choice (B)? Does this excerpt describe an object, animal, or idea using human characteristics? No. But this choice does contain a simile—it uses the word "like" to compare two things. Answer choice (B) is not correct.

What about answer choice (C)? Does this excerpt describe an object, animal, or idea using human characteristics? Can a parachute really jump off a back and run away? No, so this is an example of personification because the parachute is given human characteristics. Before you choose answer choice (C), check out answer choice (D).

Look at answer choice (D). Does this excerpt describe an object, animal or idea using human characteristics? No. But this choice does contain a simile—it uses the word "as" to compare two things. Answer choice (D) is not correct. Answer choice (C) is the best answer.

The **Know It All Approach** has helped you find the correct answer: answer choice (C). The correct answer choice has to be supported by information in the passage. Always use the information in the passage to identify the correct answer.

Kick your feet up and sit back as you focus on these passages and questions.

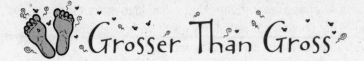

Grosser Than Gross

Funky Feet

Ever since he started to play basketball, Fred has funky foot odor. When he walks into the locker room, he is embarrassed to take off his sneakers. "My feet smell like rotten eggs!" Fred says. He imagines that his sneakers feel like vomiting from the odor.

Fred decides to talk about his problem with his cousin Kenny, who is a foot doctor.

"Foot odor is caused by sweat-eating bacteria," Kenny explains. "When the sweat on your feet attracts bacteria, you're in trouble—bacteria love to feed on your sweat. The odor in foot odor comes from the bacteria's excretion. Because your feet sweat a lot—there are more than 250,000 sweat glands in each foot that can produce a pint of sweat a day—the bacteria certainly don't go hungry. Unfortunately, shoes and socks are like a prison for the sweat on your feet. Because bacteria thrive in the dark, damp, and confined environment that your socks and shoes provide, they pig out on your sweat. The more the bacteria eat, the more they excrete waste—that's what you smell when you take off your shoes and socks."

"It smells funky," Fred agrees. "Smelly feet are a jail sentence. When I enter the locker room, I feel as if my feet have taken me prisoner. I don't want to take off my sneakers until everyone else is already in the shower. What can I do?"

"It's hard to keep your feet from sweating when you're playing sports," Kenny says. "Unfortunately, the more your feet sweat, the more your feet are going to stink. The goal is to keep your feet from sweating so much."

"The less I sweat, the fewer bacteria, which means less bacteria excretion."

"Exactly! All of which means less smell!"

"So, how do I stop my feet from sweating while I play b-ball?"

"Well, for starters, always wear clean socks, and make sure they are made of absorbent materials, like cotton. Absorbent socks are enemies of bacteria because the sock will soak up the sweat."

"Which means that the bacteria won't have anything to feed on."

"You got it. Another way to prevent foot odor is to wash your feet with antibacterial soap. It won't stop you from sweating, but it will kill bacteria. Also, give your basketball sneakers time to air after you wear them—that will help to make the sweat evaporate. Also when you're not playing basketball, try not to wear restrictive shoes. Well-ventilated shoes keep your feet from sweating so much."

"Wow. If those steps will take away my funky foot odor, I will give them a try."

"I have a feeling that you will notice a big improvement. If none of that helps, though, we will move on to step two."

"What's step two, amputation?"

Kenny laughs. "We'll hold off on amputation for now. Step two is a prescription from me to treat your funky feet."

1. Which excerpt uses personification?

A *If those steps will take away my funky foot odor, I will give them a try.*
B *I don't want to take off my sneakers until everyone else is already in the shower.*
C *The more you sweat, obviously, the more your feet will smell.*
D *He imagines that his sneakers feel like vomiting from the odor.*

2. Which excerpt uses metaphor?

A *Smelly feet are a jail sentence.*
B *What's step two, amputation?*
C *My feet smell like rotten eggs.*
D *That will lessen your bacteria load as well.*

 For Your Amusement

Seeing Double

Artie and Arnie are twins. Here in Twinsburg, Ohio at the Twins Festival Day, they are not alone. As they wait in line to sign in and get their nametags, Arnie tells the twins in line before them, "We've been twins our whole life."

"Duh," says Artie. Artie thinks Arnie is a dork.

"We are like horses of the same color," Arnie says, putting his hand around Artie's shoulder. Artie knocks it off.

"Why do you have to look like me?" says Artie. "I can't even lie and pretend that I don't know you!"

The girls before them laugh.

"I'm Barrie," the one standing by Artie says.

"I'm Bonnie," her sister, who stands by Arnie, says.

Arnie tells Bonnie and Barrie that Artie wears the *Don't Look at Me* T-shirt he has on so much that it's going to run away in search of a washing machine. Barrie and Bonnie giggle.

"He's like a bad dream that I keep having, only when I wake up he's real!" Artie says.

"Is it your first time at the Twins Day Festival?" Bonnie asks Arnie.

"Sure is," Arnie says. "I feel as if I am seeing double."

"You are," Barrie says. "We have been coming for the past few years. Our mom and her twin sister came the first year the festival began, in 1976. They grew up here in Twinsburg, Ohio."

"Twins growing up in Twinsburg—that's totally cool," says Arnie. "It's like clowns being born into a circus."

"Don't listen to him," Artie says. "He's stupid, but don't worry—it's not contagious."

Bonnie laughs. "You two are like a comedy duo."

"Hey," said Arnie. "Don't you think it's a huge coincidence that the Twins Day Festival was founded in Twinsburg?"

"Actually," Barrie says, "the event is in honor of Aaron and Moses Wilcox. They're the twins who inspired the city to adopt its name in 1817."

It's Artie and Arnie's turn to get their nametags and sign in.

"I'm Artie," Arnie says to the person writing the names down on the nametags, while his brother bends down to tie his shoelace.

He winks at Barrie and Bonnie and puts his finger to his lips.

"Shhh. Let's have some fun!"

3. Which excerpt uses personification?

A   *Here in Twinsburg, Ohio at the Twins Festival Day, they are not alone.*

B   *Artie wears the* Don't Look At Me *T-shirt he has on so much that it's going to run away in search of a washing machine.*

C   *"Actually," Barrie says, "the event is in honor of Aaron and Moses Wilcox, twin brothers who inspired the city to adopt its name in 1817."*

D   *Our mom and her twin sister came the first year the festival began, in 1976.*

4. What does Arnie mean when he says, "It's like clowns being born into a circus."

   A   that he wishes he was a clown   C   that clowns are like twins

   B   that it's a good fit   D   that it is not a good fit

Subject Review

If you met a metaphor, simile, or personification at the park, would be able to tell them from one another? This chapter was about cool dives, smelly feet, and double visions, but it was also full of useful information.

Figurative language is language or expressions that are not literally true but express some truth beyond the literal level. Figurative language appears in all kinds of writing, but it is especially prominent in poetry.

Types of figurative language called figures of speech include the following:

Metaphor: a figure of speech that compares two or more things that have something in common. In contrast to a simile, a metaphor does not use the words *like* or *as*; a metaphor implies the comparison instead of stating it directly.

Simile: a figure of speech using *like* or *as* to compare seemingly unlike things

Personification: a figure of speech in which an animal, object, force of nature, or idea is given human qualities or characteristics

Now you should be able to answer the questions from the beginning of the chapter.

"Plunging down into the Cave of the Swallows is like dropping down into an underground planet" is an example of _____?

A simile. The sentence uses the word "like" to form a comparison.

"Foot odor is enough to make a pair of sneakers want to run away" is an example of _____.

Personification. In the sentence an object—a pair of sneakers—is given human qualities or characteristics.

"Twins Day Festival is a seeing double event" is an example of _____.

A metaphor. The sentence implies a comparison.

CHAPTER 12
Point of View and Characterization

How would you describe Prince Babar?

What are "smart clothes"?

Can you laugh excess pounds away?

Now matter how you look at it, you'll learn a thing or two by completing this chapter about point of view and characterization.

Characters

A **character** is an individual in a literary work.

Main characters are the most important to a work. They are usually the heroes or protagonists in a story. **Minor characters** are less important. Like its name suggests, they play a smaller part in the story, helping or hindering the protagonist as the story progresses. You can further describe characters in the following terms:

- A **round character** shows varied and sometimes contradictory traits.

- A **flat character** reveals only one personality trait.

- A **stereotype** is a flat character of a familiar and often-repeated type.

- A **dynamic character** changes during the story.

- A **static character** remains primarily the same.

The **narrator** is a special kind of character. He or she is the person who tells the story. In some cases, the narrator is a character in the story. At other times the narrator stands outside the story.

The narrator is not necessarily the **author,** who is the person who writes the story or article or poem. Sometimes the narrator is unreliable or doesn't know the whole story. It is also possible that the narrator and the author will hold different views about the actions in the story. This is why the distinction is an important one.

Point of View

The point of view is the relationship of the narrator, or storyteller, to the story. There are numerous ways to describe point of view. Here are three common and important terms you'll need to know.

In a story with **first person point of view,** the story is told by one of the characters referred to as "I." The reader generally sees everything through the character's eyes.

In a story with a **third person omniscient point of view,** the narrator is outside the story and knows everything about the characters and events.

In a story with a **third person limited point of view,** the narrator is outside the story and reveals the thoughts of only one character, but refers to that character as "he" or "she."

Characterization

Characterization refers to the methods a writer uses to reveal the personality of a character.

- In **direct characterization,** the writer makes direct statements about a character's personality.

- In **indirect characterization,** the writer reveals a character's personality through the character's words and actions and through what other characters think and say about the character.

Meet some cool characters by checking out this example.

The Little Prince's Big Presence

Don't ever let an adult tell you that you have to wait until you get older to make your mark on the world! Prince Babar, who descended from the greatest Mongol warrior, Genghis Khan, conquered his first kingdom when he was fourteen!

Prince Babar didn't have time to go to school. He acquired his first kingdom when he was only twelve. He inherited the throne from his father. When Babar was thirteen, he led an army to Samarkand, which was a rich Central Asian city. It took seven months for Prince Babar to conquer Samarkand and become its ruler. At the time, he was only fourteen! Although his reign only lasted one hundred days, it was enough to make him fall in love with Samarkand. For many years to come, he was to conquer and lose Samarkand many times before he was finally cast out of Samarkand. For the rest of his life, even after the passionate soldier had conquered other lands that were superior to Samarkand, he still wished for his lost city of Samarkand.

Aside from being a well-known soldier, Babar was a good scholar and administrator. Whenever you feel like you are too young to make your mark on the world, think of Babar and all that he accomplished from the time he was twelve until he died thirty-seven years later at the age of forty-seven.

▶ The narrator's account of Babar shows that he _____ the young prince.

A   is not impressed with
B   despises
C   admires
D   is friends with

Now conquer the sample question using the **Know It All Approach.** Start by reading the passage carefully. Underline the words that you think are the most interesting and important. Then carefully read the question and all of the four answer choices.

What do you think about answer choice (A)? Is there evidence that the narrator is not impressed with Babar? Look back at the passage. There is no evidence that supports this point of view. Answer choice (A) is not correct.

What about answer choice (B)? Is there any evidence that the narrator despised Babar? Look back at the passage. There is no evidence that supports this point of view. In fact, the narrator is enthusiastic about Babar. Answer choice (B) is not correct.

What about answer choice (C)? Is there evidence that the narrator admires Babar? Look back at the passage. The narrator states that you should think of think of Babar and "remember that if you set your mind to something, anything is possible." There is evidence in the passage that the narrator admires Babar. Before you choose answer choice (C), take a look at answer choice (D).

Look at answer choice (D). Is there evidence that Babar is friends with Babar? Look back at the passage. Because the narrator mentions that Babar lived in the year 1497, it's unlikely that the narrator was friends with Babar. Answer choice (D) is not correct. Answer choice (C) is correct.

The Know It All Approach has helped you find the correct answer: answer choice (C). The correct answer choice has to be supported by information in the passage. Always use the information in the passage to identify the correct answer.

Make sure to be clear on the point of view of the passage or story you are reading. Ask yourself who is telling the story?

- The word "I" indicates that the story is being in told in the **first person point of view,** which means that you see everything through the character's eyes.

- If the words "he" or "she" appear in a story and you only see the story from the he or she's point of you, the story is told from a **third person limited point of view.**

- If you are told about all of the characters in a story and you are able to enter into each of their points of views, then the story is being narrated from a **third person omniscient point of view.** *Omniscient* means "all knowing." Fairy tales are often told from a third-person omniscient point of view.

Mad Science

Smart Clothes

For her fourteenth birthday, Sam wants a shirt with a mind of its own. Ever since she read about the new technology that creates shirts that act as personal information processors, she knew that she had to have one! What luck that she read the article a few weeks before her big day. There was plenty of time for her to plant seeds with her parents.

Her best friend Jess doesn't understand what the big deal is about a shirt that can monitor things about you.

"Why do you need a shirt to tell your heart rate, the temperature, and whatever else it does?"

"It's an invaluable information infrastructure," Sam says.

"Oh no, are you going all mad scientist on me again?" Jess says.

"Imagine that people were able to understand what was going on in you when you felt or thought certain things? Wouldn't it be great to have a better understanding of what you were all about? That's the idea behind smart clothes. They provide a very systematic way of monitoring what's going on inside of us without making us feel all self-conscious about being monitored."

"Huh?"

Sam laughs. She knows from her parents that she tends to get all confusing when she starts talking about science stuff. She has wanted to be a scientist since she was a little girl, but she forgets sometimes that not everyone dreams of being a scientist. She tries again.

"It's a way to learn all about what's going on inside of you without you knowing you're being monitored. It uses Interconnection Technology, and because it can be attached to shirts that are pretty cool looking, I might add, it can be worn easily by anyone from your baby sister to your grandmother!"

"Oh, sure, got it, Jess. Whatever you say."

"One day, we are all going to be wearing clothes that are equipped with Interconnection Technology."

"But why would we want to?"

"Well, think of your father. You know how some nights when he is on duty, you get nervous about him being a police officer and all? If he had on a shirt with an information system built in, people at his police department would be able to monitor his actions. Clothes with built-in information systems would also be a great way for us to observe astronauts, athletes that were competing, and soldiers. The possibilities are endless!"

"So do you really think your parents will get you one for your birthday?"

"I'm working on it! I am trying to convince them that if I had a shirt with an information system, they would always be able to track me down!"

"Yikes! Let's not mention it to my parents. If it meant they could keep tabs on me, I bet they would buy me one for my birthday too!"

1. Based on the passage, how do you think Jess feels about clothes that use Interconnection Technology?

   A confused
   B enthusiastic
   C passionate
   D bored

2. Based on the fact that the narrator is outside of the story and reveals Sam's thoughts, you can conclude that the story is narrated from

   A a first person limited point of view.
   B a third person omniscient point of view.
   C a limited third person point of view.
   D none of the above.

3. The author's account of Sam shows

   A that she loves cool clothes.
   B that she is passionate about science.
   C that she doesn't care about science.
   D that she doesn't like her friend Jess.

Laugh-a-Lot Lilly

My daughter, Lilly, laughs a lot. She even laughs in her sleep! Just the other night, I heard her laughter from my bedroom. I looked at the clock and it was almost 3:00 a.m. I thought I was going to catch her on the phone or watching a late night movie, but when I walked into her bedroom, she was sound asleep. She was having a giggling spell in her sleep! Once, Lilly fell off her bike and we rushed to comfort her. All of a sudden she had a giggling fit. I tell her about it now and she says, "Oh mom, don't get all nostalgic on me!"

Living with so much laughter led me to do some research. I wanted to know what her giggles were all about. My research discovered that the average adult laughs nearly seventeen times in one day. I learned that the reason that Lilly's laughter just keeps on going is that a sensor in the brain kicks in when you laugh and triggers a laughing response in other parts of the brain. This means laughter creates more laughter! Here's something interesting that I discovered in my investigation: humans are the only species capable of laughter.

It turns out that laughter does a body good. It reduces the levels of stress hormones in the body, which cuts down on stress. Doctors also say laughter speeds up healing by increasing blood and the oxygen flow.

The most interesting information I uncovered had to do with the fact that scientists believe that laughing can help you to lose weight! Supposedly, laughing 100 times burns up as many calories as riding a stationary bike for fifteen minutes. Laughter versus the gym? I choose laughter!

4. Based on information in paragraph 1, readers can accurately conclude that Lilly

   A   was a happy child.
   B   cried a lot.
   C   was always falling.
   D   never smiled.

5. What point of view is this story told from?

   A   third person omniscient point of view
   B   first person point of view
   C   third person limited point of view
   D   None of the above

Do you get the point about point of view and characterization? This chapter was about powerful princes, intelligent clothes, and lots of laughter, but it was also full of useful information.

Character: A character is an individual in a literary work.

Narrator: The narrator is the person who tells a story. In some cases the narrator is a character in the story. At other times the narrator is outside the story.

Author: The author is the person who writes the story or article or poem.

Point of View: The point of view is the relationship of the narrator, or storyteller, to the story.

Characterization: Characterization refers to the methods a writer uses to reveal the personality of a character.

Now you should be able to answer the questions from the beginning of the chapter.

How would you describe Prince Babar?
No, not the elephant prince of the same name! There are many terms you could use to describe Babar including courageous and ambitious.

What are "smart clothes"?
Smart clothes are clothes wired to computers, sensors, and other devices. Unfortunately, they're not yet smart enough to take you tests for you.

Can you laugh excess pounds away?
While it might not burn of the calories like a regular exercise program, laughter does burn calories.

CHAPTER 13

Conflict, Plot, Setting, and Sequence

What sorts of food do modern astronauts take into space?

What famous rock 'n' roll star was told he should stick to driving trucks because he had no future in music?

What functions do your eyebrows serve?

Stories are more than words strung together on a page. In this chapter, you'll get the full story on conflict, setting, and sequence.

Conflict

Conflict is the struggle between opposing forces in a story or play. An **external conflict** exists when a character struggles against some outside force, such as another person, nature, society, or fate. An **internal conflict** exists within the mind of a character that is torn between opposing feelings or goals.

Plot

Plot is the sequence of events in a narrative work. The plot begins with **exposition,** which introduces the story's characters, setting, and conflicts. The **rising action** adds complications to the story's conflicts, or problems, leading to the **climax,** or **turning point,** which is the moment of highest emotional pitch. The **falling action** is the logical result of the climax; the **resolution,** sometimes called **denouement,** presents the final outcome.

Sequence

Sequence is the progression of events in a story. The plot unfolds through a sequence of events.

Setting

Setting is the time and place in which the events of a story, novel, or play occur. Setting includes the ideas, customs, beliefs, and values of the time and place. The setting often helps create an atmosphere, or mood.

Here are some tips on answering questions involving conflict, sequence, and setting. First, if you are unsure about the importance of an event in the story, look back at the passage. Usually, if you note the reaction of a character to that event, you can get an idea of what role that event plays in the conflict.

Second, as you read, pay attention to the sequence of events in the story in order to see the relationship among different events in the story. This will help you to interpret the plot more effectively.

Now check out the story on the next page and engage in the age-old conflict of reader versus sample question.

Outer Space Oddities

Corned Beef in Space!

In 1965, at 9:24 in the morning, a Titan-II rocket lifted into space. On its nosecone it carried the Gemini 3 spaceship and astronauts, Virgil "Gus" Grissom and John Young, into orbit. The mission objectives included testing out Gemini's two-man design, checking new space equipment NASA had packed into the Gemini capsule, and, finally, to take numerous photographs of Earth from orbit. The capsule was packed with all the necessary scientific and photographic equipment and, it turns out, a little something extra. John Young was carrying one corned beef sandwich.

Back in the early days of space exploration, the food astronauts received for their flight left much to be desired. Most of it was dehydrated, which turned whatever the meal was meant to be into a gritty dust. Astronauts were supposed to rehydrate their meals by mixing the dust together with cold water in a squeeze tube. If you wonder what this tasted like, imagine eating steak-flavored toothpaste. The food was the way it was for specific reasons. First, the food was lightweight and easily stored. Second, and perhaps more importantly, the paste left behind no crumbs. This may seem like a small thing, but crumbs float in the weightlessness of space. Floating around unchecked, these crumbs could jam up sensitive computers and controls. Still, most astronauts hated the food. It was for this very reason that Young snuck on his own in-flight meal.

During the course of the flight, without telling mission control what they were doing, Grissom and Young split the corned beef sandwich. Fortunately, both were careful eaters and no crumbs seem to have escaped into the machinery of the Gemini capsule. However, avoiding disaster wasn't enough to keep the two astronauts out of hot water. When NASA and the press discovered that the astronauts risked their lives and the capsule for a sandwich, a massive controversy was kicked up. NASA spokesmen told the press that steps would be taken "to prevent corned beef sandwiches in future flights."

To ensure no more crumby sandwiches would pop up in future space missions, NASA set about making better meals for the astronauts. Modern astronauts eat meals that are pretty much like the food they would get on Earth. They are served in TV dinner style trays and heated and re-hydrated in a specially-designed cover.

But, according to Michael Collins, NASA still won't allow corned beef sandwiches in space.

▶ Which of the following best describes the main conflict in the story?

   A   Astronauts don't like to work in pairs.
   B   Astronauts snuck dangerous food onto the Gemini capsule.
   C   Astronauts make bad photographers.
   D   The only thing astronauts will eat is corned beef.

Satisfy your hunger for knowledge by figuring out the answer to the sample question. Use the **Know It All Approach.** Start by reading the passage carefully. Underline the words that you think are the most interesting and important. Then carefully read the question and all of the four answer choices.

What do you think about answer choice (A)? Does the conflict in the story revolve around the fact that *astronauts don't like to work in pairs*? Look back at the passage. Although the passage mentions that the Gemini capsule was a two-man ship, there is no indication that the astronauts did not enjoy working together. Answer choice (A) is not correct.

What about answer choice (B)? Does the conflict revolve around the fact that the *astronauts snuck dangerous food onto their ship*? In the story we see that the astronauts snuck a sandwich onto the capsule. Was this dangerous? The passage tells us that the crumbs from the sandwich could have jammed up onboard computers and controls. That's very dangerous! This appears to be the correct answer, but before you make a decision, check out the remaining answer choices.

What about answer choice (C)? Are the astronauts *bad photographers*? The passage says nothing about the astronauts' photographic skills. You may happen to be an expert on the history of space exploration and may, somehow, know that the photographs the Gemini 3 astronauts took were of poor quality because the lens on their camera was set wrong. Still, this information is not in the passage. When you are finding the answer to a reading passage question, rely on the information in the passage and try to put any extra details you may happen to know aside. Answer choice (C) is not correct.

Read answer choice (D). Does the conflict revolve around the fact that *the only thing astronauts will eat is corned beef*? Look back at the passage. Although the astronauts took a corned beef sandwich on board, there is nothing that says the only food an astronaut will eat is corned beef. Answer choice (D) is not correct. Answer choice (B) is the correct answer.

Now shake, rattle, and roll into these passages and questions.

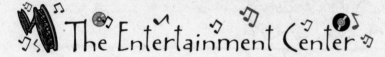
The Entertainment Center

The King is Born

Singing came naturally to the young choirboy Elvis Aaron Presley. His parents bought him an acoustic guitar and, by listening to old spiritual and blues tunes, he taught himself how to play. Presley's family moved to Memphis, Tennessee in 1949, just before he entered high school. After graduation in 1953, Elvis earned a living driving a truck for the Crown Electric Company and enrolled in evening classes in order to become an electrical repairman.

Even though he had a day job, the young Elvis continued to pursue his singing career. It's a good thing that he didn't listen to the advice of Jimmy Denny, manager of the Grand Ole Opry. After one performance, Jimmy fired the young Elvis. Rumor has it that Jimmy told Elvis to give up on music and return to his truck driving job, "because you're never going to make it as a singer."

This setback, of course, was not the end of Elvis' music career. After the loss of his Grand Ole Opry job, Elvis had stopped by a local music studio to make a small two-song disc as a gift to his mother. A copy of the disc found its way to Sam Philips, president of Sun Records. Upon hearing the disc, Philips believed he had found the next singing sensation.

The rest is pop music history. Elvis recorded numerous albums, appeared on television shows and in films, and toured around the globe. His success not only helped to establish rock 'n' roll as a profitable musical genre, but also inspired future artists and paved the way for them.

1. Which of the following provides the events in the passage in the correct order concerning Elvis's road to stardom?
    A   choir boy, graduates high school, plays the guitar, moves to Memphis
    B   moves to Memphis, choirboy, plays the guitar, graduates high school
    C   high school, plays the guitar, choirboy, moves to Memphis
    D   choirboy, plays the guitar, moves to Memphis, graduates high school

2. Which of the following occurred first in the passage?
    A   Elvis was a choirboy.   C   Elvis was discovered by Sam Philips.
    B   Elvis was a truck driver.   D   Elvis recorded songs for his mother.

Above the Eyes

For her tenth grade sociology project, Olivia has decided to study eyebrows. Her studies at the school library have taught her that eyebrows help keep unwanted moisture out of our eyes. When rain or sweat drips down our foreheads, the eyebrows shield our eyes and redirect the flow. For her project, Olivia is focusing not on how eyebrows help to shield us, but on how eyebrows help us express emotion. Olivia's hypothesis is that by looking at a person's eyebrows, you can determine just how they feel.

First, Olivia observed her family members' eyebrows, but she knew their expressions too well and studying their eyebrows bored her. She was about to abandon her topic and pick something new until she notices the eyebrow activity, or rather inactivity, of her neighbor, Mrs. Huber. No matter if she smiles or frowns with the rest of her face, Mrs. Huber's eyebrows sit still.

"Is something on my face?" Mrs. Huber said when Olivia said hello to her.

"No, nothing," Olivia said. "Don't mind me."

"You're looking at me strange," Mrs. Huber says.

"Oh, I just put drops in my eye," Olivia says. "They're blurry."

"Okay, then. Have a great afternoon." She seems happy, Olivia thought, but her eyebrows just sit in a straight line. They don't move.

Olivia decided to do some investigative research on Mrs. Huber. She knew Mrs. Huber always prepared dinner at 5:00 p.m. With that in mind, she positioned herself outside Mrs. Huber's kitchen window. She was determined to find out if Mrs. Huber's eyebrows ever moved.

Mrs. Huber sings as she chopped up onions and then tomatoes for a salad. When she looked in the refrigerator, Olivia saw a frown on her face, and still, her eyebrows didn't move! How can it be? Mrs. Huber's eyebrow inactivity defied Olivia's hypothesis!

Just as Olivia was about to write down her findings, Olivia dropped her pen. She ducked, but it is too late. Mrs. Huber spotted her out the window. Mrs. Huber's eyes opened in wide-eyed surprise. And still, her eyebrows didn't budge!

"Olivia!" she said. "What are you doing child? Snooping on me, were you?"

"It's not what you think, I can explain." But could she?

"Please do!"

"Well, see, I am doing this project for school. It's on eyebrows."

"A project on eyebrows. Oh, I think I get it."

"Your eyebrows disproved my hypothesis that you can read a person's emotions by their eyebrows. I was looking in on you to find out if your eyebrows ever moved."

Mrs. Huber laughed. "I think I can help you to understand why my eyebrows don't move. When I was a little girl, I had an accident. I had surgery across my brows. As a result, that part of my face is numb."

"So, do eyebrows express a person's feelings?"

"They sure do, just not mine."

Olivia had an idea. "Could I interview you to find out if not having expressive eyebrows make a difference in your life?"

"Sure thing," Mrs. Huber said.

3. Which of the following occurred first in the passage?

A Olivia decides study eyebrows.
B Olivia observes her family's eyebrows.
C Mrs. Huber catches Olivia snooping outside.
D Olivia talks to Mrs. Huber on her porch.

4. Which of the following characteristics of the setting are important for the events in the passage to take place?

A that Olivia lives in a house
B that Olivia is outside after school
C that Olivia studies at the library
D that Olivia lives next door to Mrs. Huber

5. What is the sequence of events in the passage? Use details from the passage to support your answer.

_____

_____

_____

_____

Subject Review

Do you know it all about conflict, plot, sequence, and setting? This chapter was full of space brownies, singers on their way to stardom, and brow-raising stories, but it was also full of useful information.

Conflict is the struggle between opposing forces in a story or play.

- An **external conflict** exists when a character struggles against some outside force, such as another person, nature, society, or fate.

- An **internal conflict** exists within the mind of a character that is torn between opposing feelings or goals.

Plot is the sequence of events in a narrative work. The plot begins with an **exposition,** which introduces the story's characters, setting, and conflicts. The rising action adds complications to the story's conflicts, or problems, leading to the **climax,** or **turning point,** which is the moment of highest emotional pitch. The falling action is the logical result of the climax; the **resolution,** sometimes called **denouement,** presents the final outcome.

Sequence is the progression of events in a story. The plot unfolds through a sequence of events.

Setting is the time and place in which the events of a story, novel, or play occur. Setting includes the ideas, customs, beliefs, and values of the time and place. The setting often helps create an atmosphere, or mood.

Now you should be able to answer the questions from the beginning of the chapter.

What sorts of food do modern astronauts take into space?
Modern astronauts take up normal meals that are served in TV dinner style trays. It might not be a great meal, but it must be better than eating out of a tube.

What famous rock 'n' roll star was told he should stick to driving trucks because he had no future in music?
Elvis Presley was told he had no future in music.

What function do your eyebrows serve?
You could answer this question two ways. You could say they protect your eyes from sweat and moisture. You could also say that they help express emotions.

Impact!

It's a good thing for us here on Earth that Jupiter was our bodyguard when the Shoemaker-Levy 9 comet struck in the summer of 1994. Jupiter's southern hemisphere took quite a blow when the fierce comet crashed into it—more than twenty fragments of the comet shook Jupiter! The largest, simply called fragment G, struck Jupiter with the force of 6,000,000 megatons of TNT. Scientists estimate that this is nearly 600 times the destructive capacity of all the nuclear armed nations arsenal combined. When fragment G hit the surface of Jupiter, a giant fireball rose 3,000 kilometers into the sky. That's roughly the distance from Washington, D.C., to the Utah/Nevada border.

It's not every day that a comet storms through the sky threatening a collision. In fact, there are scientists who await such events, and carefully monitor them. Such was the case with Shoemaker-Levy 9. Astronomers Carolyn and Eugene Shoemaker, and David Levy discovered the forceful comet the year before it struck. This enabled them to predict the consequences of the collision.

It was the threesome's discovery along with the technology of the Hubble Space Telescope and the Galileo interplanetary probe that enabled astronomers around the world to observe the comet-planet collision for the first time ever. For six days during July 1994, astronomer's observed fragments from the comet barraging Jupiter, causing gigantic fireballs in Jupiter's atmosphere. A number of the fragments that attacked Jupiter left splotches in the planets sky that were more than double the size of Earth!

1. Which excerpt below is an example of metaphor?

   A   *the comet-planet collision*

   B   *Jupiter was our bodyguard*

   C   *fragments from the comet barraging Jupiter*

   D   *discovered the forceful comet*

2. How do you think that the author feels about astronomers who monitor comets?

   A   grateful

   B   hateful

   C   disappointed

   D   excited

3. Based on the fact that Jupiter had fireballs in its atmosphere because of fragments of the Shoemaker-Levy 9's bombarding it, what can you conclude about the comet? Use details form the passage to support your answer.

   _____

   _____

   _____

   _____

   _____

4. Which of the following best describes the astronomers who discovered the comet before it struck?

   A   They were dedicated astronomers.

   B   They didn't care much for their jobs.

   C   They were excited to photograph the comet.

   D   They were alarmists who wanted to scare people.

5. Which of the following occurred first in the passage?

   A   Jupiter exploded into the atmosphere.

   B   Jupiter hid behind the earth to avoid the blow.

   C   Shoemaker-Levy 9 comet struck.

   D   Fragments bombarded Jupiter for six days.

CHAPTER 14
Cause and Effect

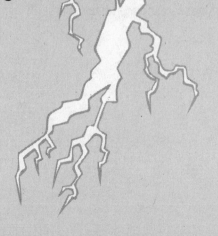

Why did Christy Brown write a book about his life?

What was the result of John Gayetty's invention?

Why did "Afraid of Crowds" write to Dr. Drip?

ecause you are reading this book, you are becoming a real know it all. Get a smart start to full know it all status by completing this chapter about cause and effect.

Cause and Effect

Cause is the reason why something in a story or poem or article happens. It helps you to understand the relationship between events in the story.

Effect is the result that stems from the thing that happens.

To answer cause-and-effect questions, you should be aware of how certain events in a story influence other things in a story, such as a decision a character makes. When looking for cause and effect relationships in a passage look for the word "because." The word "because" is helpful in understanding cause-and-effect relationships because it makes a connection between the cause and effect.

Remember that the answer choices you select should always be based on information that you read in a passage. Although some answer choices may seem correct based on your general knowledge of the events described, those answer choices are probably incorrect if you can't support them with information directly stated in the passage.

There will always be enough information in the passage to figure out the cause or effect of something that happens in the story. When you write out answers for an open-response item, be sure to use specific information from the story that highlights the cause-and-effect relationship that you are asked about.

As always, don't hesitate to return to a passage to look for key words. This could remind you of important details in the passage concerning cause-and-effect relationships. Key words can help you to gather specific information to write your answer to an open-response item.

The cause: you want to learn more. The effect: you read this example!

 Art-rageous

Portrait of an Artist as a Left Foot

Writing with your left foot is probably not something you do in your free time. Perhaps Christy Brown wouldn't have tried it either, if his circumstances were different. But he was diagnosed at a very young age with cerebral palsy. Caused by damage to the brain, cerebral palsy results in speech impairment and lack of muscle coordination. In Brown's case, he couldn't control his speech or muscle movements, except for his left foot. The doctors thought Brown was helpless and hopeless, even mentally defective. But Brown's mother knew his mind was fine, even though his body was not. With twelve other children to raise, she still refused to give up on Brown.

One day, when Brown was five, he picked up a piece of his sister's chalk with his left foot. With great effort, and to the amazement of his family, he wrote the letter "A." Now his mother knew for sure that her son's mind was intact, and she decided to become his teacher. She taught him to write the alphabet with his left foot, letter by letter. Soon he learned how to sign his initials and then write his entire name. Brown was determined to communicate with the world. It was as if his left foot had a mind of its own! It wasn't long before he began creating art with his left foot. At the age of twelve, one of his paintings won a children's painting competition.

As Brown grew up, his writing matured too. He eventually wrote his beautiful and inspirational autobiography, *My Left Foot*. Brown's tale of perseverance, and his desire to communicate despite the body that imprisoned him, is a reminder to us all that if there is a will, there is always a way to overcome hardship.

▶ Why did Christy Brown begin to write with his left foot?

A Because he could not write with his hands.
B Because he liked to be different.
C Because he liked to pick up chalk with his foot.
D Because his mother asked him to write with it.

Show what you know by figuring out the answer to the sample question using the **Know It All Approach.**

Start by reading the passage carefully. Underline the words that you think are the most interesting and important.

Next, carefully read the question and all of the four answer choices.

What do you think about answer choice (A)? Did Brown write with his left foot because he *could not write with his hands*? Look back at the passage. It states that Brown could not control his muscle movements, so you can assume that he could not control his hands. Before you choose answer choice (A), read the other answer choices.

What about answer choice (B)? Did Brown write with his left foot *because he was creative and original*? Reread the passage. We are not told that Brown liked to be different. Answer choice (B) is not correct.

What about answer choice (C)? Did Brown write with his left foot *because he liked to pick up chalk with his foot*? Reread the passage. While Brown may have liked to pick up chalk with his left foot, that information is not supplied in the passage. Answer choice (C) is not correct.

Look at answer choice (D). Did Brown's mother ask him to write with his left foot? Look back to the passage. It says nothing that would support this answer. Answer choice (D) is not correct. Go back to answer choice (A). Answer choice (A) is correct.

The **Know It All Approach** has helped you find the correct answer: answer choice (A). The correct answer choice has to be supported by information in the passage. Always use the information in the passage to identify the correct answer.

Now you're on a roll. Try these passages and questions.

Private Matters

While Joseph Gayetty may not be a household name, chances are you're very familiar with his invention. In 1857 this ingenious New Yorker produced the first packaged toilet paper in the United States. His toilet paper was made of flat, stacked sheets of unbleached paper, and each piece was printed with Joseph Gayetty's name. The product was marketed as "therapeutic paper," and a package of five-hundred sheets sold for about fifty cents.

Although Gayetty may have been among the first to create such a toilet product as we know it, the use of toilet paper dates back more than one thousand years. Its first documented use was in China. Paper, however, was not the only material used to get the job done. The public toilets of the early Romans included a sponge on a stick that was kept on hand in a bucket of seawater. In other cultures, the wealthy classes used wool, cotton, or even lace to wipe away their waste. What royal treatment! By contrast, people in lower classes had to use whatever came to hand. Rumor has it that colonial Americans favored leaves or corncobs in their outhouses.

It's easy to see why Gayetty's invention was a welcome one. Most Americans at that point had grown accustomed to using torn-up newspapers and catalogues. The *Sears Catalogue,* printed on porous paper, was the most popular "personal paper" of choice. Taking Gayetty's lead, the Scott Paper Company marketed the first toilet paper in rolls. The company was founded in Philadelphia in 1879 by the two Scott brothers, who launched their "unmentionable" tissue-roll product around 1890. Not much has changed since then, and chances are we'll be rolling along with this invention for a long time to come.

1. What most likely caused Gayetty to invent paper for the toilet?
   A   He wanted to look through the *Sears Catalogue* and not use it in the bathroom.
   B   He was no longer pleased with corn cobs.
   C   He was tired of using the roll of toilet paper that the Scott brothers invented.
   D   He wanted sanitary paper to use when he went to the bathroom.

2. Which of the following resulted from the Scott brothers' invention?
   A   a roll of toilet paper
   B   sheets for the toilet
   C   more paper for the toilet
   D   alternatives for wealthy people

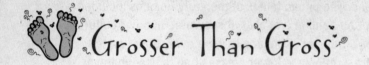 **Grosser Than Gross**

According to Dr. Drip

Dr. Drip knows all there is to know about sweating. Read his weekly question and answer column to find answers to all of your sweating uncertainties!

Dear Dr. Drip,

I sweat buckets when I exercise. I notice at the track that some people who run beside me don't even shed a drop of sweat. Does this mean I'm in terrible shape?

Signed,

Sweataholic

Dear Sweataholic,

It's a myth that people who sweat a lot are out of shape. In fact, the opposite is true! As your body gets in better shape, it adapts to cool itself more efficiently. The sweat glands learn to increase production of their sodium, or salty, fluid, which cools the body as it evaporates from the pores of the skin. This allows your glands to release more water and cool down your body more effectively. As your fitness level increases, you sweat earlier in your exercise phase, and you sweat more. More sweat is actually a good thing, because it decreases your chances of overheating.

Dear Dr. Drip,

Why do I sweat more in closed spaces full of people?

Signed,

Afraid of Crowds

Dear Afraid of Crowds,

A room full of warm bodies makes the surrounding temperature and humidity increase significantly. Your body in this situation retains more heat, and you sweat more. Because the room is filled with people, there is little airflow, and it decreases the rate at which sweat can evaporate from your skin or (or dry from your clothes!). That's why it seems like you are sweating more; sweat drips off you as liquid rather than evaporating into the air. The more people you pack into a small space, the more likely you are all to glisten with sweat.

Dear Dr. Drip,

Do we sweat when exercising in water?

Signed,

Fish

Dear Fish,

Whether you exercise indoors, outdoors, or in water, if you become hot enough you'll sweat. Even though you don't notice the sweat, you still cool off (as long as the water is cooler than your body temperature). Your body's extra heat simply transfers from your skin to the water. Even if you can't tell that you've been sweating because you're in the water, it's still important to replace the fluids you've lost by drinking plenty of water.

3. According to the passage, what is the reason why people sweat more in closed spaces full of people?

    A   Heat is mainly lost through direct body contact with the water via conduction and convection.
    B   As your fitness increases you sweat sooner and sweat more and, as a result, face less risk of overheating.
    C   Low airflow and high humidity reduces the rate at which sweat evaporates, making it even harder for you to dissipate heat.
    D   Your sweat glands respond to exercise by becoming larger, allowing them to release more water and thus cool down your body more effectively.

4. What caused Fish to write to Dr. Drip?

    A   Fish was afraid to swim lately and wanted to know why.
    B   Fish wanted to know if he sweats while exercising in water.
    C   Fish believed that sweat was weighing him down in the water.
    D   Fish wanted to know why people smelt bad while swimming.

5. Sweathaholic wrote to Dr. Drip because

    A   she was afraid that she was losing too much water.
    B   she sweats more than others while running track.
    C   she doesn't sweat as much as others sweat at the track.
    D   she wants to learn how to sweat more when she runs.

Subject Review

Are you a whiz at determining cause and effect? This chapter was full of talented feet, toilet paper tales, and dripping doctors, but it was also full of useful information.

Cause is the reason why something in a story or poem or article happens. It helps you to understand the relationship between events in the story.

Effect is the result that stems from the thing that happens.

Now you should be able to answer the questions from the beginning of the chapter.

Why did Christy Brown write a book about his life?
So that he could share his experiences of communicating with the world by way of his left foot.

What was the result of John Gayetty's invention?
We can use toilet paper instead of corn cobs!

Why did "Afraid of Crowds" write to Dr. Drip?
He wanted to know why he sweats more in closed spaces full of people.

CHAPTER 15
Using Graphic Organizers

What health benefits do you get from eating onions and garlic?

Who was the first American woman astronaut?

What is the largest spider in the world?

*S*eeing is believing. Not convinced? Learn all about it by completing this chapter about graphic organizers.

Graphic Organizers

Graphic organizers help you reconstruct ideas in a visual way, so you can remember them later on. You might make a **chart** or **diagram,** showing the information the author provides.

Venn diagrams help you to map out a comparison and contrast text structure. The outer portions of the circles will show how two characters, ideas, or items contrast, or are different, and the overlapping part will show how they are similar, or compare them.

Flow charts help you keep track of the sequence of events. Arrange ideas or events in their logical, sequential order. Then, draw arrows between your ideas to indicate how one idea or event flows into another.

A **web** will help you to determine a main idea and supporting details. Surround the main idea with examples or supporting details. Then create additional circles, branching off from the supporting details, to add related thoughts.

Here are some tips for using visual organizers and answering visual organizer questions.

- When you are comparing or contrasting ideas or characters in a passage, it helps to list comparisons and contrasts in an orderly way. That will help you to see what characters or ideas have in common and how they differ.

- When you are looking for similarities between characters or ideas, the following words are triggers: *similarly, like*, and *in the same way*. When you are looking for differences between characters or ideas, the following words or phrases are triggers: *however, although, in contrast, on the other hand*, and *unlike*.

- Labeling paragraphs is a great way to keep track of the sequence of events in a passage. Also, it can be useful to list events in the order in which they appear in the passage. Then number each event as it occurred in the passage, with labeling the first event "1." This will let you see how the author has designed the time sequence of a selection.

- The first and last paragraphs of a passage often provide important clues about its theme or main idea. When you are trying to figure out the main idea or theme of a passage, look for clues in three places: the title, the first paragraph, and the last paragraph.

Satisfy your taste buds by checking out this example.

Food Folklore

Aviva and Gina love to share their food folklore facts with anyone who will listen. They make a good team, considering that Aviva only shares information about the foods that she loves, and Gina, who likes different food from Aviva, only shares information about the foods that she loves. There is one food, though, that they both love. Speaking of the food fact girls, tune in below to hear them for yourself.

Aviva: Carrots are super for your eyes. The beta-carotene in them can reduce the chance of eye disease.

Gina: Carrots are gross! But, did you know that chicken soup fights congestion that comes with a cold? If you want to unstuff yourself, eat some chicken soup! It has a protein in it that thins the lining of the sinuses, and relieves annoying stuffiness.

Aviva: Chicken soup is for wimps! Now garlic and onions—they're intense. They kill flu and cold viruses.

Gina: Garlic and onions make for stinky breath! If you want to get smart, then what you need is fish. Fish is fantastic for your brain. The mineral zinc is found in fish and shellfish. If you are lacking in zinc, according to some studies, your thinking and memory may be impaired.

Aviva: Fish is for fishermen. How about sweet, settling blueberries? Yum. They fight bacteria that can cause stomach upset.

Gina: Blueberries look like gerbil poop. Bananas, on the other hand are not only sweet and satisfying, but they are a natural antacid. That means that if you are in distress from heartburn or gastric issues, you should reach for a banana.

Aviva: Bananas make me feel like vomiting! But spinach—totally awesome stuff. Not to mention that it's good for your spirits. It contains lots of folic acid. If you are feeling depressed, it just may be that your body doesn't have enough folic acid.

Gina: Spinach is for Popeye. What we all need is some ginger. Ginger fights nausea and helps relieve annoying headaches.

Aviva: Ginger hurts my taste buds. What we all need is some soothing yogurt. Yogurt fights bacteria that cause infections.

Gina: Yogurt is yummy. And to think it fights bacteria! Totally awesome stuff!

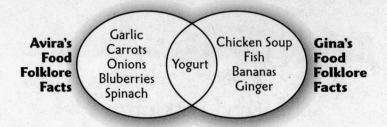

Avira's Food Folklore Facts: Garlic, Carrots, Onions, Bluberries, Spinach

Yogurt

Gina's Food Folklore Facts: Chicken Soup, Fish, Bananas, Ginger

▶ Based on the information in the Venn diagram, which of the following statements would be true?

A   Aviva likes fish.
B   Gina likes garlic and onions.
C   Aviva and Gina both like chicken soup.
D   Gina likes ginger.

Now answer to the sample question using the **Know It All Approach.**

Start by reading the passage carefully. Underline the words that you think are the most interesting and important. Then carefully read the question and all of the four answer choices.

What do you think about answer choice (A)? Does Aviva like fish? Look at the Venn diagram for easy reference. Aviva does not like fish according to the diagram. Answer choice (A) is not correct.

What about answer choice (B)? Does Gina like garlic and onions? Look at the Venn diagram for easy reference. Gina does not like garlic and onions. Answer choice (B) is not correct.

What about answer choice (C)? Do both Aviva and Gina like chicken soup? Look at the Venn diagram for easy reference. According to the Venn diagram, only Gina likes chicken soup. Answer choice (C) is not correct.

Look at answer choice (D). Does Gina like ginger? Look at the Venn diagram for easy reference. According to the Venn diagram, Gina does like ginger. Answer choice (D) is correct.

The **Know It All Approach** has helped you find the correct answer: answer choice (D). The correct answer choice has to be supported by information in the passage. Always use the information in the passage to identify the correct answer.

Strap in tight and get ready to take off with these passages and questions.

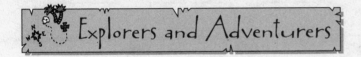

Women in Space

For her midterm project, Michele plans to write a report on women in space. She found out that the first animal in orbit, a Russian dog named Laika, was female. Laika, whose name meant "Barker" in Russian, was launched into space in 1957. Laika, however, was not exactly the sort of thing Michele had in mind. She wanted to write about the women explorers and scientists who had journeyed to space. Before she writes her report, she wants to organize how she will share the information she has gathered in the library. She thinks it's best to write the report in a chronological order, starting with the earliest information that she has found. In order to organize her research, Michele intends to create a flow chart.

Check out the information she's found and help her to make a flow chart.

- In 1999, on STS-93 on the Columbia space shuttle, Eileen Collins became the first woman space shuttle commander.

- On March 11, 2001, American astronaut Susan Helms made a record-breaking space walk. Her walk lasted 8 hours and 56 minutes, and succeeded in breaking the old record by 30 minutes.

- In 1983, Sally Ride, the first American woman astronaut, became a member of the space shuttle's seventh mission.

- In 1963, Valentina Tereshkova was the first woman in space. Taking off from the Tyuratam Space Station in the Vostok VI, Tereshkova orbited Earth for almost three days. Her journey proved that women had the same resistance to space as men.

- In February 1992, Mae Jemison became the first African American woman in space.

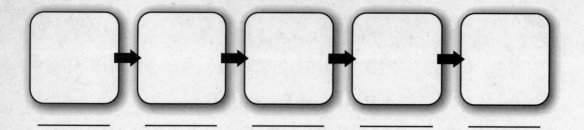

——————— ——————— ——————— ——————— ———————

1. Based on the research above, if Michele is to write a report that details facts in chronological order, what is the correct sequence? Use the boxes above to help you to chart the correct chronological order of events.

   A 5, 3, 4, 1, 2
   B 2, 1, 3, 4, 5
   C 1, 2, 5, 3, 4
   D 5, 4, 3, 2, 1

2. What information belongs in the third box?

   A *On March 11, 2001, American astronaut Susan Helms took a record-breaking space walk.*
   B *In February 1992, Mae Jemison became the first African American woman in space.*
   C *In 1999, on STS-93 on the Columbia space shuttle, Eileen Collins became the first woman space shuttle commander.*
   D *Valentina Tereshkova was the first woman in space.*

The Web of the Goliath Bird-Eating Spider

Are you afraid of spiders?

Many people find even the smallest arachnid unsettling, but maybe you're braver than that.

How about an eleven inch long spider? That's most likely longer than the distance between your elbow and your wrist. Still feeling brave?

The enormous spider in question is the goliath bird-eating spider of South America. A resident of the lush rain forests of the northeastern Amazon, these outsized members of the tarantula family are the largest spiders in the world. The largest on record possessed an eleven inch leg span.

Like other spiders, the goliath bird-eating spider is a predator that must eat other animals to live. However, unlike many of the spiders you may be used to, it does not spin a web to catch flies. It must stealthily hunt down its prey, pounce, and deliver a venomous bite to its victim with its one-inch long fangs. After it has subdued the victim with poison, it drags the victim to it lair or a nearby safe hiding spot. The spider does not have any teeth to devour its prey with. Instead, it regurgitates digestive fluids onto its victim. These digestive acids breakdown the victim, much the same way food is broken down in your stomach—only the spider digests its food before it eats it! Once the acids have dissolved the victim, the spider sucks up its prey through a straw-like feeding tube. After a goliath bird-eating spider has finished its meal, the only traces of the victim left are the bones and fur or feathers.

The goliath bird-eating spider's name isn't just for show. The bird-eater rarely eats an adult bird, but they have been know to sneak into a nest while mother bird is away and snatch hatchlings for food. However, this is not the main source of food for the bird-eating spider. The majority of the spider's diet consists of frogs, small snakes, beetles, and the occasional bat.

Despite its fearsome appearance and crude table manners, the goliath bird-eating spider does not pose a threat to humans smart enough to leave it well alone. While the spider's venom is more than enough to incapacitate its normal prey, it is not deadly to humans. If you are bitten by a bird-eating spider, the bitten area will swell up and hurt for a few hours, not unlike a bee sting. It won't be pleasant, but it won't kill you.

If the idea of a swollen bite wound doesn't convince you to stay away, the bird-eating spider has a second line of defense hidden in its fur. When threatened, the bird-eating spider can release tiny, nearly invisible, irritating hairs into the wind. If these hairs get on your skin, a rash is the least they'll do. Serious damage can occur if the hairs get in your eyes or are breathed into your throat and lungs.

Luckily, it is easy to stay way from the aggressive bird-eating spider. Unlike most spiders, the bird-eating spider makes noise when feels threatened. Rubbing together stiff bristles on its legs, the bird-eating spider can create a loud hissing sound. The spider's hiss can be heard up to fifteen feet away.

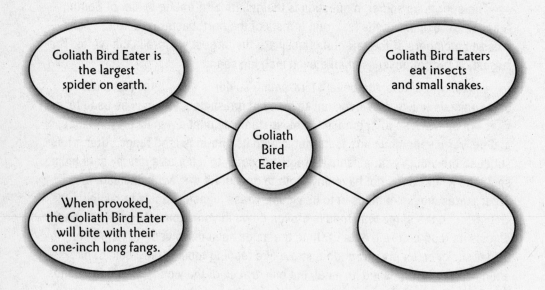

3. What is the main idea of the passage?

    A   The goliath bird-eating spider is the largest spider in the world.
    B   The goliath bird-eating spider is venomous.
    C   The goliath bird-eating spider releases painful hairs when alarmed.
    D   The goliath bird-eating spider eats insects and small reptiles.

4. Which of the following phrases belongs in the empty circle?

    A   The Amazon rain forest is in South America.
    B   Birds sometimes leave hatchlings in the nest unattended.
    C   Bee stings cause swelling that can last for hours.
    D   Goliath bird-eating spiders flick painful hairs when alarmed.

5. What is the purpose of the graphic organizer for this passage?

    _____

    _____

    _____

    _____

6. The circle describing the diet of the goliath bird-eating spider is missing some information. What would you information for the article would you add to circle to complete the graphic organizer?

    _____

    _____

    _____

    _____

Subject Review

Are you an expert at organizing information? This chapter was full of fun food facts, adventurous women, and scary spiders, but it was also full of useful information.

Graphic organizers help you reconstruct ideas in a visual way, so you can remember them later on. You might make a chart or diagram, showing the information the author provides.

Venn diagrams help you to map out a comparison and contrast text structure. The outer portions of the circles will show how two characters, ideas, or items contrast, or are different, and the overlapping part will show how they are similar, or compare them.

Flow charts help you keep track of the sequence of events. Arrange ideas or events in their logical, sequential order. Then, draw arrows between your ideas to indicate how one idea or event flows into another.

A **web** will help you to determine a main idea and supporting details. Surround the main idea with examples or supporting details. Then create additional circles, branching off from the supporting details, to add related thoughts.

Now you should be able to answer the questions from the beginning of the chapter.

What health benefits do you get from eating onions and garlic?
Onions and garlic kill flu and cold viruses.

Who was the first American woman astronaut?
The first American woman in space was Sally Ride. She flew on the space shuttle in 1983.

What is the largest spider in the world?
Measuring up to eleven inches long, the goliath bird-eating spider is the biggest spider of them all.

CHAPTER 16

Using Informational Resources

If you wanted to find out more about the International Grand Champion Whistler, where would you be most likely to find more information?

Who was Wonder Woman's father?

Which hairs make for a softer toothbrush: hog hairs or horse hairs?

Before you write another report, become a super researcher by completing this chapter about using informational resources.

Using Informational Resources

Informational resources are valuable tools to use when you are writing a report for school, or if you're just interested in learning more information about a specific subject. For instance, after reading a passage in *Know It All!* about emoticons, you may be inspired to learn more about emoticons on your own. Knowing about the different informational resources available would help you to know where to go to satisfy your desire to *know it all* about a topic. Read about these informational resources.

An **almanac** is a publication containing astronomical and meteorological data for given years. It contains yearly statistical, tabular, and general information. For instance, you would look in an almanac to learn the predicted temperature and rainfall for the state of Kentucky next summer, or how many inches of rain fell there in July 1888.

An **atlas** is a bound collection of maps. It often includes illustrations, information tables, and textual matter as well. You would consult an atlas for geographical locations and information on various cities, states, and countries. You could look in an atlas to find the quickest route from New York City to Florida, or to learn that Des Moines is the capital of Iowa.

A **dictionary** is a reference book containing alphabetically listed words and their meanings. It also contains information on the forms, pronunciations, and functions of the words, along with their origins, syntaxes, and idiomatic uses. You would consult a dictionary to find out how to spell a word, or to learn if a word is even a word, such as when you're playing *Scrabble™.* Some dictionaries offer explanations on usage rules with words that are often confused, such as "which" and "that."

An **encyclopedia** is a work that contains information on all branches of knowledge. Some of these branches include science, world history, literature, biography, geography, and the arts. Comprised of many volumes, an encyclopedia is usually arranged by subject matter and the individual articles about the subjects are arranged alphabetically. You would consult an encyclopedia to learn about the life of Dr. Martin Luther King, Jr. or to find out if certain tree frogs can actually fit on the tip of your finger.

A **magazine** is a periodical containing various pieces of writing such as articles, stories, and poems. It is often heavily illustrated and contains advertising. Magazines fall into many categories such as academic, trade or commercial, and business to business. Magazine subjects can range from medical research to fashion, literature to photography, and computers to house plants. You would look in *Newsweek* magazine, for example, to learn about current events.

A **newspaper** is a periodical that is distributed on a regular, frequent basis, usually daily or weekly. It contains local and international news, opinion articles, and feature stories, as well as listings for things like cars for sale or apartments for rent. You would read a newspaper to learn the latest news, find out the weather report, or look for a job.

A **thesaurus** is a book of words and their synonyms. You would consult a thesaurus to find an alternate word for one you had already used in the same context. For example, if you are writing an e-mail to your parents describing the great time you're having in California, the word "awesome" might appear several times. To avoid repetition, you could look up "awesome" in the thesaurus and add "amazing" and "wonderful" in its place.

A **primary resource** is a firsthand account of an event by someone who has actually experienced or observed the event. A primary resource could be an autobiography or a news article by a journalist.

A **secondary resource** is one that is written by a person who has done extensive research on the topic using primary sources. The secondary source often involves a certain amount of interpretation of the topic. Although most sources on a topic will be secondary, you should make use of primary resources when they are available.

Begin your quest for knowing by checking out this example.

Bizarre Human Feats

Whistle While You Work

The next time someone asks you to please stop whistling, tell them you're "the next Steve Herbst in training." Then, if they look at you strangely, you can explain that Steve Herbst is a celebrated grand-champion whistler!

As both a "musical" entertainer and a competitive whistler, Steve Herbst takes whistling seriously. He has performed at Carnegie Hall and the Kennedy Center for the Performing Arts, as well as on numerous national television programs, such as *The Today Show* and *CNN*.

In 2002, Herbst brought his competitive lips to Louisburg, North Carolina, for the annual International Whistlers Competition. He won first place as the International Grand Champion Whistler in the classical category and took second place in the popular music category. The following year, he was honored with the prestigious title, "International Whistling Entertainer of the Year," the most coveted award in this form of entertainment.

Born into a musically inclined family, Herbst decided to make his lips his instrument at a very young age. He would practice intensely to develop his whistling skills, like anyone learning to play an instrument such as the piano or violin. Today, he not only wins competitions and appears on television, but he draws people to follow him, pied-piper style, as he walks along the busy sidewalks whistling his brilliant tunes.

Whistling as an art form, however, is still not widely accepted. As Herbst explains, "The challenge is getting people to appreciate whistling as I do is being a musician." If people would actually try to create beautiful music by whistling, they would realize how difficult it actually is and appreciate it more. So start practicing. You never know what musical beauty may eventually flow out when you pucker your lips and blow. You just may be the next whistling phenomenon!

▶ This article would most likely be found in a magazine called

A   *The Importance of Vocal Cords*
B   *Sounds from Above*
C   *Unusual Talents and Awards*
D   *People Who Don't Make Noise*

Make some noise of your own to figure out the answer to the sample question using the **Know It All Approach.**

Start by reading the article carefully. Underline the words that you think are the most interesting and important. Then carefully read the question and all four answer choices.

What do you think about answer choice (A)? Would this article be found in a magazine called *The Importance of Vocal Cords*? Because the article is about whistling, not singing or talking, chances are that the passage would not be in this magazine. Answer choice (A) is not correct.

What about answer choice (B)? Is this article likely to be found in a magazine called *Sounds from Above*? Although the sound of whistling could come "from above," such as from a high window, this title is very general. Continue to the rest of the answer choices to see if there is a better answer.

What do you think about answer choice (C)? Is this article likely to be found in a magazine called *Unusual Talents and Awards*? Chances are the answer is yes. Steve Herbst's talent and the awards he won for it are certainly unusual compared to regular musical talent and competitions. Before you select answer choice (C), however, make sure there is not a better one. Check out answer choice (D).

Look at answer choice (D). Would this article be likely to be found in a magazine called *People Who Don't Make A Lot of Noise*? Because it is about whistling, chances are that the article would not be in this magazine. Answer choice (D) is not correct. Answer choice (C) is the best answer.

The **Know It All Approach** has helped you find the correct answer: answer choice (C). The correct answer choice has to be supported by information in the passage. Always use the information in the passage to identify the correct answer.

Now get ready for wondrous adventures by reading these passages and questions.

 Art-rageous

Wonder Woman, Wonder Man

Wonder Woman, with her gold, red, and blue costume, is one of the most recognizable pop culture icons ever to leap of the pages of comics books. And while her strange adventures and unusual powers may seem odd to the uninitiated reader, they pale in comparison to the uncanny story creator of the sensational superhero.

Wonder Woman was the brain child of the eccentric Harvard trained inventor and pop-psychologist William Moulton Marston. Even before he started inventing superheroes, Marston lived an unusual life. Born in 1893, in Cliftondale, Massachusetts, Marston took his law degree in 1918, and went on to receive his doctorate in psychology from Harvard in 1921. He taught college courses in Washington, D.C., for a few years and then served briefly as the director of public services for Universal Studios in California. Never one to rest on his laurels, he also invented the "systolic blood-pressure test," and an early version of the modern lie detector, and wrote several books on psychology for the non-professional reader. In these books he put forth a few controversial theories. He claimed that men were inherently violent and anarchic, and that women were a civilizing influence who could bring modern culture into an ideal state of "loving submission." Furthermore, he felt that it was the future of human civilization to become a matriarchy, or a culture ruled by females.

Although Marston's views were not widely adopted, his interest in feminism and his strong distaste for what he saw as the negative impact of gender stereotypes on the development of young girls self-esteem made him a popular figure in the world of comic publishing. In 1940, Marston took the post of "educational consultant" for Detective Comics (later simply DC Comics). When he arrived at Detective Comics, heroes like Batman and Superman dominated the comic world. Sensing a need for a positive role model for young women, Marston suggested the creation of a female superhero. Under the pseudonym "Charles Moulton," Marston submitted a story idea featuring a heroine named Suprema. The Surpema name was dropped in favor of the now-familiar Wonder Woman, and the new heroine made her first appearance in *All Star Comics 8.* She was a hit and, by the summer of 1942, newsstands were selling *Wonder Woman 1.*

Throughout the years, Wonder Woman continued to be a female symbol of truth and strength through the decades. In 1972, she was featured on the cover of Ms Magazine's first issue. In 1986, however, the *Wonder Woman* was briefly cancelled, but reader demand brought it back. Despite his many achievements, Wonder Woman has proven to be Marston's most enduring achievement.

1. If you wanted to find more information about this topic, you would be most likely to find it in which of the following resources?

   A   a dictionary
   B   an encyclopedia
   C   an atlas
   D   a newspaper

2. This passage would most likely be found in a collection called

   A   *Famous Women in History.*
   B   *Cartoon Super Heroes.*
   C   *Landmarks in Modern Psychology.*
   D   *Famous Inventors of the Twentieth Century.*

Know It All! High School Reading

Tales of Tooth

Hogs hair and your teeth are two topics you wouldn't be likely to talk about in the same sentence. But back in the fifteenth century, people used toothbrushes whose bristles were made from the backs of Siberian hogs! Understandably, many people found the hog bristles too stiff and abrasive on the gums and chose to stick with toothpicks to clean their teeth and gums, while others preferred softer horse or badger hairbrushes to clean their teeth.

Pierre Fauchard, who in 1728 wrote *The Surgeon Dentist,* a standard work on dentistry, recommended the use of natural sponge to clean teeth. Goodbye hog bristle toothbrushes! In 1938, Dupont introduced toothbrushes with nylon bristles to replace pig hair. One can only imagine how grateful brushers were.

Gross or not, it's a good thing that the hog toothbrush surfaced back in the fifteenth century. Not only did the invention undoubtedly help bad breath, but according to a survey by the Massachusetts Institute of Technology in 2003, the toothbrush took top honors as the one invention that the nation cannot do without. The toothbrush beat out automobiles, computers, and cell phones! Apparently, people are serious about their toothbrushes!

3. In a library, *Tales of Tooth* would most likely be in which of the following sections?
   A   current events
   B   biography
   C   history
   D   literature

4. Which of the following encyclopedia headings would be **least** likely to provide information that relates to this article?
   A   "Modern Procedures to Fill Cavities"
   B   "Dental Care in the Fifteenth Century Versus Now"
   C   "Fifteenth Century Inventions That Have Endured"
   D   "The Various Uses of Hog Hair in the Fifteenth Century"

Subject Review

Do you know where to go to find information? This chapter was full of whistling sensations, a woman of wonder, and toothbrush tales, but it was also full of useful information. Remember to use the following informational resources to help you to do research.

- An **almanac** is a publication containing astronomical and meteorological data for a given year. It also contains yearly statistical, tabular, and general information.

- An **atlas** is a bound collection of maps often including illustrations, informative tables, or textual matter. It contains tables and charts regarding cities, states, and countries.

- A **dictionary** is a reference book containing words alphabetically arranged along with information about their forms, pronunciations, functions, etymologies, meanings, and syntactical and idiomatic uses.

- An **encyclopedia** is a work that contains information on all branches of knowledge or treats comprehensively a particular branch of knowledge usually in articles that are arranged alphabetically.

- A **magazine** is a periodical containing miscellaneous components, such as articles, stories, and poems; it is often illustrated.

- A **newspaper** is a paper that is printed and distributed usually daily or weekly and that contains news, articles of opinion, features, and advertising.

- A **thesaurus** is a book of words and their synonyms.

- A **primary resource** is a firsthand account of an event by someone who has actually experienced or observed the event.

- A **secondary resource** is one written by a person who has done extensive research on the topic and who has interpreted primary sources.

Now you should be able to answer the questions from the beginning of the chapter.

If you wanted to find out more about the International Grand Champion Whistler, where would you be most likely to find more information?

You could find more info about the champion whistler in a newspaper or a magazine article.

Who was Wonder Woman's father?

Feminist, scholar, author, and inventor William Marston created Wonder Woman.

Which hairs make for a softer toothbrush: hog hairs or horse hairs?

Apparently horse hairs are softer on the gums, but I'll stick with nylon fibers thank you.

WILD CARDS

Sticky Matters

Making chewing gum isn't something you can do at home. But, if you've ever wondered what goes into the chewy little treat, you can walk thought the steps right here.

In order to make your own chewing gum, first you'll need a gum base. The gum base is a inert, insoluble base. That may sound complicated, but any gum chewer knows what the gum base is. When you chew gum so long that all the flavor is gone, what your left with is the gum base. Once you've got a gum base, you'll need some sweeteners. Sugar, corn syrup, and whatever flavors you want in your gum will act as the sweeteners. You may want to add softeners to your list of ingredients. This will prevent your gum from turning into a hard little rock before you get to chew it. Glycerin and vegetable oil will work just fine to soften your gum. Once you have all the ingredients, you will need to decide which type of gum you plan to make. Different gums require different recipes. If you want to make bubble gum, for example, you better load up on the gum base. The gum base lets the gum stretch without tearing and is the reason you can blow bubbles without having them pop immediately.

No two gums are made exactly the same way, but some of the basic steps are always the same. The process is a bit tedious, but we all know how worthwhile the results are! Ready for the first step in the process? You will need to prepare the gum base. The raw gum materials need to be melted down in a steam cooker. After that, your base will go for a spin in a high-powered centrifuge. The centrifuge spins the gum around and around so quickly, the traces of bark and dirt that are common to raw gum go flying off the gum base. Once the melted gum base is clean, you will need to combine the ingredients. No two gums are the same, but here is a rough approximation of what's in the gum you can buy at the local candy store: 20 percent gum base, 63 percent sugar, 16 percent corn syrup, and 1 percent flavoring oils. While the mixture is still warm, you will need to run the mixture between rollers that are coated with powdered sugar. The powdered sugar helps to keep the ribbons of gum from sticking to each other. Using knives or an automated cutting machine, you cut the gum into strips, cubes, or whatever shape you want. That's what you will need to cut the ribbon into sticks of gum. Once the sticks of gum are ready, it's time to wrap them!

Chewing gum gets a bad rap from teachers and parents who don't like the smacking sounds or the sight of students blowing bubbles when they should be paying attention to their lesson. But that's only half the story. Chewing gum helps to clean your teeth. The act of chewing helps stimulate saliva production. This added moisture washes away tooth decay causing acids before they can build up on your teeth and do serious damage. Chewing gum also helps people to concentrate and stay awake. If you feel uptight, reach for a stick of gum. Chewing gum is known to help ease tension and to relax people. So next time you get hassled for chewing gum, hand the uptight critic a stick and tell them to relax.

1. According to the article, the reason that bubble gum contains more of the gum base, is

   A   to make the gum sweeter tasting.
   B   so that your bubbles don't burst.
   C   to helps to clean the teeth.
   D   to clean the melted gum base.

2. If you were to chart how to make gum in a flow chart, which step would come first?

   A   snipping the ribbon into sticks
   B   clean the melted gum base
   C   rid the gum base of undesirable dirt
   D   the raw gum materials be melted down

3. This passage would most likely be found in a collection called

   A   *How to Keep Your Braces Intact*
   B   *The Facts About Your Favorite Treats*
   C   *Vegetable Trivia You Want to Know*
   D   *How We Digest Food We Eat Every Day*

4. In a library, this passage would most likely be in which of the following sections?

   A   science
   B   mystery
   C   biography
   D   social studies

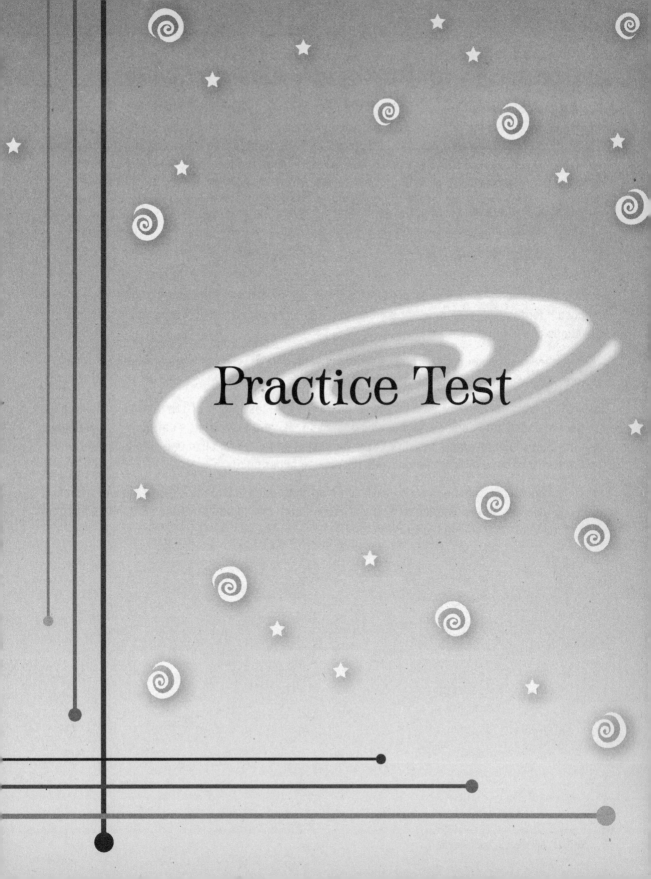

Practice Test

Introduction to the *Know It All!* Practice Test

By now you've reviewed all the important skills that you should know for middle school reading. You know the difference between fact and opinion (chapter 4). You recognize the handful of important literary and poetic devices (chapters 9 and 10). You learned about the major elements to a story (chapter 13). And these are just a few examples that don't even include all the excellent tidbits of information you've picked up. You Know It All!

If you're ready, it's time to try out the skills from the sixteen chapters in this book in a practice test. This test may be similar to a test you take in class. It contains both multiple-choice and open-response questions.

The multiple-choice questions on the test have four answer choices. You should bubble in the correct answer choice on a separate bubble sheet. Cut or tear out the bubble sheet on page 179, and use it for the multiple-choice questions. You can write your answers to the open-response questions directly in the test.

The practice test contains thirty-one questions, twenty-five of which are multiple choice. Give yourself ninety minutes to complete the test.

Take the practice test the same way you would take a real test. Don't watch television, don't talk on the telephone, and don't listen to music while you take the test. Sit at a desk with a few pencils, and have an adult time you if possible. Take the test in one day and all in one sitting. If you break up the test in parts, you won't get the real test-taking experience.

When you've completed the practice test, you may go to page 205 to check your answers. Each question also has an explanation to help you understand how to find the answer. Don't look at this part of the book until you've finished the test!

Good luck!

Sample Questions

Directions

Read each passage. Then read the question that follows the passage. Choose the best answer to each question. On the answer sheet provided at the end of the practice test, mark the letter of the correct answer choice.

The Interview

      Thomas, an intern at the magazine *Music Notes* couldn't believe his luck. He was going to interview singer/songwriter Willie Nelson! His hands quivered. He hoped he would be able to write. The intern that turned in the best interview would get the summer position at the magazine.

      Thomas checked the notes he'd made in preparation for the interview. He already knew that Nelson sold the copyright for his first song for a mere $150. He'd bought a second-hand car with the cash and drove to Nashville hoping to break into country music.

      Thomas's boss interrupted his thoughts. "Are you all set for the interview?" his boss asked. "Do you know what you are going to ask Mr. Nelson?"

      Thomas took a deep breath. He knew that his boss believed in him and was counting on him to get the full-time position by turning in the best interview. "I'm all set," he said. He looked down at his hand, which was steady now. "I can't wait to talk to Mr. Nelson!"

▶ From the passage, you can tell that *quivered* means

  A   shook.
  B   kept still.
  C   waved.
  D   tingled.

▶ The intern that got the full time after-school position at the magazine would be the one to turn in—

  A   the best interview
  B   the best song
  C   the best boss story
  D   the best day dream

The practice test passages and questions will begin on the following page.

The Endurance

On August 1, 1914, the artic explorer Ernest Shackleton and his crew left London in their polar exploration ship, *The Endurance,* headed for Antarctica. Shackleton's goal was to cross the Antarctic continent. What he didn't know when he started out was just how prophetic his ship's name was.

The expedition started well enough. Shackleton was a little worried when the ship encountered ice well north of its usual position. This was a sign that the winter would be unusually cold, although few of the crew thought it would be dangerously so. There was also a brief panic when the ships captain, Frank Worsley, fell through some thin ice while playing soccer with some crew members. Worsely was rescued and the crew returned to their duties shaken, but still determined.

As the mission continued, the weather got worse and worse. Shackleton and his crew were faced with one of the coldest artic winters on record. The ice accumulated around *The Endurance* and, by January 19, the ship was completely trapped. Rather than panic, Shackleton and his crew began to plan for long-term survival. At first, they believed that they could survive on the ship just fine. Then, in October of that same year, the horrible discovery was made: *The Endurance* was slowly sinking! The men abandoned ship and set up temporary camp on the nearby ice. Packed so deeply in the ice, it took nearly a month for the ship to sink. On November 21, *The Endurance* slipped underneath the snow and ice, gone forever.

Although the men dreamed of being rescued, a rescue party never materialized. In time, the ice surrounded the men melted, and once again, there was running water. With Schackleton leading them, the men sailed away in lifeboats that they had saved from the ship. The men arrived on Elephant Island after battling stormy seas. Unfortunately, they were far from civilization, which meant to them that they would die either of starvation or from the cold. A brave Shackleton refused to let his men die. Gathering his bravest men, Shackleton and his selected few set sail on the lifeboat *James Caird.* For seventeen days, with enormous waves threatening them and ice-cold weather numbing them to the bone, the group sailed until they ultimately reached South Georgia Island.

With limited resources to navigate, the journey was far from easy. After crossing huge mountains, the group discovered a whaling station. Finally, they were able to organize a rescue team for the crewmembers that they had left behind on Elephant Island! It took another three months for the rest of the men to be rescued.

Two years after they started out, the entire crew was safe and back home. Shackleton's leadership and bravery was crucial in saving all of his men.

1. What does the word *materialized* mean in paragraph 4?

    A   showed up
    B   disappeared
    C   lost them
    D   sailed away

2. Shackelton's left London because he

    A   took pleasure in sailing in bad weather.
    B   wanted to be the captain of *The Endurance*.
    C   wanted to cross the Antarctic continent.
    D   wanted to go on a long journey.

3. This passage is an example of

    A   satire.
    B   drama.
    C   biography.
    D   poetry.

4. The main purpose of this passage is to

    A   prove that *The Endurance* really existed and set forth in 1958.
    B   provide details about the ship that Shackleton sailed.
    C   share the amazing story of Shackleton and his crews' survival.
    D   scare people to never try to cross the Antarctic continent.

5. What is the tone at the end of this passage?

    A   pessimistic
    B   humorous
    C   ironic
    D   reverential

6. Suppose you wanted to write an article arguing that Ernest Shackleton was a brave man. What information in this passage could you use to support your argument? Include details and information from the passage in your response.

_____

_____

_____

_____

_____

_____

_____

_____

_____

_____

_____

_____

_____

_____

_____

_____

_____

Speed

Some days I wish more than anything that I could just go faster. I will be on my bike, riding home from school and I will imagine revving up my bike and suddenly moving faster than I can pedal. Then, I will have to stop at a red light, and I will be reminded that I am just riding my bike that doesn't go very fast at all.

If I were granted a wish to do anything in the world, I would ask to drive the world's fastest land vehicle: the Thrust Super Sonic Car, or Thrust SSC for short. In 1997, Thrust SSC set the first supersonic land record of 763.035 mph in the Black Rock Desert, Nevada. That same year, the Super Sonic Car became the very first land vehicle to exceed the speed of sound! I know because I read everything there is to read about Thrust SSC.

If you are used to traveling at 50 or 60 mph with your parents on a highway, you will have to buckle in tight for a ride in the Thrust SSC-or risk getting whiplash! How does it the SSC manage to move so fast? Unlike the normal cars we're used to seeing out on the streets, the SSC has two turbo jets, one on each side of the car, that power it to record breaking speeds. The two jet engines are incredibly powerful: the Thrust SSC has as much power as 145 Formula 1 race cars. How's that for speed?

Still not impressed? Despite the weight of the SSC (the car tips the scales at one ton), it can accelerate from zero to 100 miles per hours in just four seconds. That's about as much time as you probably took reading that last sentence! This car goes so fast, normal breaks would be useless. Instead, the SSC has parachutes which open up behind the car when the driver wants to stop. These parachutes catch the wind and bring the car to a stop. This means that once the SSC starts up, there are only two speeds: faster and stop!

If I hit the gas and accelerated, it would take me, oh, less than a minute to get to school in the Thrust SSC. That means that I could sleep later each morning. I know, keep dreaming! Sadly, I might never get the chance to drive the SSC. Now that it has demolished all the land speed records, and is unlikely to be beat by some other car anytime soon, there are no plans to run the super speedy car again. Currently, it is in the Museum of British Road Transport in the United Kingdom. But, if they ever want to dust of the SSC and need a driver, I'd happily volunteer!

7. In which of the following sources of information would you be LEAST likely to find information on Thrust SSC?

A *The Big Book of World Records*
B *Family Car Buyer's Digest*
C the "Science" section of a newspaper
D an encyclopedia

8. Which of the following BEST summarizes the information in the passage?

A The narrator intends to be the next person to drive the Thrust SSC.
B The Thrust SSC is the first car to use two turbojets.
C The Thrust SSC is the world's fastest land vehicle.
D The Thrust SSC has the equivalent power of 145 racecars.

9. Read this sentence from the passage.

If you are used to traveling at 50 or 60 mph with your parents on a highway, you will have to buckle in tight for a ride in the Thrust SSC or risk getting whiplash!

What does the sentence mean?

A The Thrust SSC travels at a speed much faster than what you are used to traveling.
B Be careful: the Thrust SSC does not offer a smooth ride to its riders.
C A ride in the Thrust SSC often causes people to have stiff necks.
D If you drive the Thrust SSC, you need to be sure that you wear a neck brace.

10. Based on the passage, what information supports the idea that if the narrator hit the gas and accelerated in the Thrust SSC, it would take him less than a minute to get to school in the Thrust SSC?

A The SSC uses parachutes to stop the car.
B The SSC is currently on display in a museum in the United Kingdom.
C The Thrust SSC weighs one ton.
D The Thrust SSC accelerates quickly.

11. Describe the narrator's tone in the passage. Support your answer with details and specific information from the passage.

_____

_____

_____

_____

_____

_____

_____

_____

_____

_____

_____

_____

_____

_____

_____

_____

_____

_____

_____

_____

_____

_____

_____

_____

Who's That Girl?

In art history class, we have been studying Leonardo da Vinci. I can look at his Mona Lisa every day, and still notice something new about the texture of the painting, the expression on his model's face. Our teacher told us that, while there is a lot of controversy over who the woman in Leonardo da Vinci's Mona Lisa is, no one knows for sure who modeled for the portrait.

I decided to do some investigating of my own. After going through some books in the library, I was no closer to solving the mystery of the Mona Lisa's identity, but I did gather up a few suspects.

Some art historians think that the mysterious, smiling woman may be Mona Lisa Gherardini, wife of a rich Florentine silk merchant. In fact, so many people think she's the model that we call the painting the Mona Lisa. It's actual title, *La Joconde*, is hardly used outside of art historian circles. But the case isn't so easily solved. The original source for this idea was a da Vinci biographer by the name of Giorgio Vasari. He never saw the painting in question, so art historians are skeptical of his claims.

If it wasn't Mona Lisa Gherardini, then who else could it be?

It could be nobody. Yup, it's true—that's one of the candidates for the painting. Some historians believe that the smiling woman in the painting is simply a figment of da Vinci's imagination. The historians who like this theory differ as to whether da Vinci mixed the features of numerous women together into a single picture or simply made it all up. Either way, the historians think searching for a real-life, historical Mona Lisa is a waste of time.

Finally, the strangest of all theories is that da Vinci himself is the real Mona Lisa! A weird as it may sound, some researchers think that the painting is a portrait of the artist as a woman. This theory received support in 1987, when some computer scientists compared a self-portrait da Vinci did in 1518 with the Mona Lisa. Using scanned computer images, the scientists flipped the 1518 self-portrait and overlaid it with the Mona Lisa. The researchers felt the comparisons between the two pictures were too strong to ignore.

There are many other suspects for real Mona Lisa, but the final answer to her identity will most likely remain eternally shrouded in mystery. Da Vinci, who left plenty of records about all of his other famous works, left no records for the Mona Lisa. Besides da Vinci, only one other person would know for sure who posed for the Mona Lisa, and she isn't talking.

12. Read the following sentence from the passage.

Our teacher told us that, while there is a lot of controversy over who the woman in Leonardo da Vinci's the Mona Lisa is, no one knows for sure who modeled for the portrait.

What does *controversy* mean in this sentence?

A   confused
B   debate
C   uncertainty
D   belief

13. According to the passage, how did the narrator's interest in da Vinci's Mona Lisa begin?

A   She read an article about Leonardo da Vinci.
B   She is studying Leonardo da Vinci in art history class.
C   Her teacher is interested in the Mona Lisa.
D   She is a painter and she aspires to be like Leonardo da Vinci.

14. In which sentence from the passage does the narrator acknowledge the doubt surrounding da Vinci's painting being a portrait of Mona Lisa Gherardini?

A   What we do know is that it's likely that the Mona Lisa was one of da Vinci's favorite works.
B   Unlike all of his other creations that were sold on commission, the Mona Lisa was not sold.
C   Art historians, however, now doubt that she was the model because the source of this rumor was Giorgio Vasari, da Vinci's biographer who never even saw the painting!
D   Rumor has it that in 1987, computer scientists reversed the image of da Vinci's painting, enlarged it and juxtaposed it against the Mona Lisa.

15. Which of the following BEST describes the narrator's tone?

A   curious
B   bored
C   excited
D   annoyed

16. Which of the following is the main idea of the passage?

   A   Leonardo da Vinci painted a lot of portraits of women.
   B   We may never know the identity of the woman in the Mona Lisa.
   C   Leonardo da Vinci knew a lot of women who wanted to be Mona Lisa.
   D   Some folks believe that the painting is a feminine self-portrait.

17. What is the debate that the narrator discusses in the passage? Is there any resolution to the debate? Support your answer with details and specific information in the story.

   _____

   _____

   _____

   _____

   _____

   _____

   _____

   _____

   _____

   _____

   _____

   _____

   _____

   _____

   _____

   _____

Striking Gold

On September 12, 1857, the *SS Central America*, en route to New York, sank somewhere off the coast of South Carolina. Many of the passengers where gold miners who, after striking it rich in the California Gold Rush, were now headed back east with their new found wealth. While more than 150 of the passengers were saved, the prospectors' gold was lost to the sea. When the *SS Central America* went down, it took nearly $1.6 million (1857 value) into the deep with it. This included the famed Eureka Bar, an eighty-pound gold brick with an 1857 value nearly of $17,500. In modern dollars, the Eureka Bar alone was worth $8,000,000.

The wreck of the *Central America* sank nearly 8,000 feet below the surface. Its depth and uncertain location meant that any recovery attempt made in the nineteenth century, before deep sea diving methods were invented, would be pointless. Nearly a century later, the *Central America* and the vast treasure locked deep in its wrecked hull was still considered a lost cause. At least, it was considered a lost cause by everybody except engineering student Thomas "Tommy" Thompson and geologist Bob Evans.

Convinced that modern technology could recover the *Central America,* they set out to solve the mystery of the gold ship's location. Using historical records, including newspaper interviews with survivors of the wreck, they pieced together an accurate picture of the ship's last moments. They fed this data into a computer, which could narrow down the area they would need to search. Unfortunately for the treasure hunters, the best the computer could do was narrow the search area to a section of ocean about the size of Rhode Island. Still, Thompson and Evans were determined to not give up.

In 1986, Thompson and a crew of modern day treasure hunters went to the sea to scan the area in which the computer radar said the *Central America* was located. They found numerous promising sites, including another wreck that contained numerous nineteeth-century artifacts of great importance to historians. But no gold ship!

Worried that other treasure hunters may have heard what they were up to, Thompson's crew continued on into winter, while Evans returned to their research to see if they missed some important details. While reviewing the radar scans, Evans suggested that the recovery crew check out a previously overlooked site on their way out to the deeper, more promising sites. He didn't expect it to yield much, but it would give the recovery crew a chance to test out Nemo, the recovery robot Thompson had built for the mission.

The recovery crew agreed and they stopped at Evans's proposed site. Nemo went deep into the darkness of the cold and churning Atlantic. The robot traveled for hours before it finally reached the ocean floor. It found the wrecked and silent hull of the *SS Central America*.

After a long legal battle, Thompson, Evans, and their crew recovered and claimed the gold. They did not keep all of it, though. Thompson and Evans had decided at the beginning on the treasure hunt that the gold was not just a personal resource, but rather a national treasure. The treasure hunters have provided museums, libraries, and other public collections with numerous rare gold coins and other important artifacts.

18. Read the following sentence from the passage.

They found numerous promising sites, including another wreck that contained numerous nineteenth-century artifacts of great importance to historians. But no gold ship!

What does the word *artifacts* mean in this sentence?

A discarded things
B expensive items
C used goods
D objects from the past

19. What event happened first?

A The treasure hunters fought a long legal battle.
B The treasure hunters researched the historical records.
C Nemo, the recovery robot, found the wreck of the *Central America*.
D The treasure hunters scanned a section of the ocean floor with radar.

20. Which of the following best describes Thompson and Evans?

A pessimistic
B greedy
C easily discouraged
D persistent

21. Which of the following statements BEST describes what happens in the passage?

A The *SS Central America* sinks and it treasures were lost.
B The *SS Central America* was found and the treasures were recovered.
C The underwater robot reached the bottom of the sea.
D The treasure hunters chartered an old Louisiana mud boat.

22. Suppose you wanted to write your own article about the *SS Central America*. What information from this passage could you use to write your own article? Where would you go to find more information about this event? Include details and information from the passage in you response.

_____

_____

_____

_____

_____

_____

_____

_____

_____

_____

_____

_____

_____

_____

_____

_____

_____

_____

_____

_____

_____

_____

_____

_____

Party Time

Mardi Gras, which means "Fat Tuesday" in French, is party time in the city of New Orleans, Louisiana. The name of this wild, citywide festival gives you a hint of the festival's cultural origins. Mardi Gras was a European festival that French explorers and settlers brought to America in 1699. Among the early French settlers, Mardi Gras was celebrated at home. Locals would gather at a single house and hold a masked ball. Eventually these gatherings grew so large that revelers would fill the streets. In 1718, Spanish rule came to New Orleans and dancing in the streets was prohibited. Once again, Mardi Gras became a private party. However, in 1827 Americans gained control of Louisiana, and Mardi Gras partiers were free to return to the streets.

Originally, the festival was charged with religious significance. The festival is held on the night before Ash Wednesday. Ash Wednesday, in the Christian religious calendar, marks the beginning of Lent. Lent is a traditional period of penitence and fasting observed by Roman Catholic, Eastern Orthodox, and some Protestant churches. Mardi Gras was a sort of "final" blowout before the solemn period of Lent began. The religious origins of the festival are still in evidence today. The official colors of Mardi Gras, for example, are purple, gold, and green. These colors, selected in 1872, stand for justice, power, and faith.

Although Mardi Gras is technically a religious occasion, nowadays it is more of a non-stop secular party complete with festive parades. In fact, in the four parishes of Jefferson, St. Bernard, Orleans, and St. Tammany, more than seventy parades take place. If you are thinking of attending, the best place to watch one of these parades is St. Charles Avenue.

The people behind the party are members of groups know as *krewes*. The first krewe connected to Mardi Gras was the "Mystik Krewe of Comus." This somewhat secret organization formed in 1857 and charged itself with preserving the Mardi Gras tradition. In their honor, all the groups involved in Mardi Gras are all known as krewes. Modern Mardi Gras krewes are often well-known civic organizations who want to help continue the Mardi Gras tradition and view their participation as an important service to the city. Krewes ride in full costume on ornamented floats in the many parades. They toss out strings of beads, or *throws,* to the clamoring crowds. The tradition of tossing out beads throws dates back to 1871, when a person dressed as Santa Claus tossed gifts to the crowd. This seasonally out of place Santa started a trend. Mardi Gras attendees now scream, dress up, and engage in all sorts of shenanigans in order get the krewes attention and catch some of these colorful, but worthless, beads.

23. Consider the following sentence form the passage.

Krewes ride in full costume on ornamented floats in the many parades.

What does the word *ornamented* mean in the sentence?

A   interesting
B   decorated
C   unattractive
D   enthusiastic

24. According to the passage, Fat Tuesday, or Mardi Gras occurs on the night before what event begins?

A   the parade
B   Lent
C   Easter
D   New Year's Day

25. Based on the information in the passage, what do people collect during Mardi Gras?

A   throws
B   coupons
C   masks
D   krewes

26. Which statement from the document BEST summarizes the Mardi Gras celebration?

A   Mardi Gras is the traditional festival of New Orleans.
B   Krewes perform an important service to the community.
C   The Spanish colonial government did not allow dancing in the streets.
D   People celebrate Mardi Gras by holding masked balls in their homes.

27. What is the author's tone in this passage? Support your answer with details and specific information from the passage.

_____

_____

_____

_____

_____

_____

_____

_____

_____

_____

_____

_____

_____

_____

_____

_____

_____

_____

_____

_____

The Ten Most Wanted

The Federal Bureau of Investigation (FBI) has a wealth of crime fighting tools at its disposal. Its agents are highly trained, it has offices in every state and in many foreign countries, and in its laboratories, the latest technologies are used to solve crimes and hunt down some of the most dangerous criminals ever known. Despite the wealth of talent and all the powerful technology, one of the FBI's most powerful tools against crime remains the Ten Most Wanted Fugitives list. This regularly updated list of the ten most dangerous or elusive criminals has been helping the FBI track and capture suspects and fugitives since the start of the program in March 1950.

Given the success of the program, it may come as a surprise to find out that the FBI did not come with idea for a Ten Most Wanted Fugitives list. Similar lists have existed before, most notably, the Chicago Crime Commission's 1930 list of "public enemies." Facing a rise in gang-related activity, the nonprofit citizen's group decided to publicly air the name of suspected gangsters in the hopes that the sudden notoriety would force them to curtail their criminal activities. There were twenty-eight names on the list. Before the FBI introduced their Ten Most Wanted Fugitives list, the "public enemies" list was the most famous who's who of American criminals. The top gangster on the list was Joe Aiello, leader of the bootlegging Moran Gang. Infamous gangster Al Capone was fourth on the list. The list caught the attention of Americans nationwide. In fact, the list was so popular, that it added the phrase "Public Enemy #1" to the American lexicon.

Popular as it was, the Chicago Crime Commission's list was not the direct inspiration for the FBI's Most Wanted List. Instead, that credit belongs to the International News Service. In 1949, an enterprising reporter thought it would be interesting to create a story on the most dangerous criminals the FBI was hunting. He asked the FBI to provide him with ten names for his story, and in response the FBI sent along the names of ten wanted criminals. The story was published and it turned out to be a huge hit with the public. FBI Director J. Edgar Hoover took notice of the story's popularity. Fugitives on the run need anonymity to stay hidden. Providing the public with a regularly updated list of wanted fugitives would make it harder for fugitives to remain anonymous. In 1950, Hoover officially began the FBI's Ten Most Wanted program.

The current list is built by gathering up names from the fifty-six national and international FBI field offices. From the submitted names, fugitives are selected for the list only if the FBI feels that the fugitive is especially dangerous and that the added publicity would help the case. Once a name is on the list, there are only three ways it can be removed. A fugitive gets off the list if they are caught, the charges against them are dropped (this has happened seventeen times in the history of the list), or the FBI decides they no longer pose a serious threat to the public.

Over the years the list has undergone changes. In the early days of the list, bank robbers and car thieves regularly made this list. As the scope of the FBI's activities increased, the range of criminals on the list has grown. Now the international list includes members of South American drug cartels and members of foreign terrorist organizations. What hasn't changed is the lists effectiveness. Since it began in 1950, 458 fugitives have appeared on the list. Of those, 429 have been apprehended.

28. Consider the following sentence from the passage.

Fugitives on the run need anonymity to stay hidden.

What does the word *anonymity* mean in this sentence?

A   honesty
B   incompetence
C   confusion
D   secrecy

29. Which of the following statements is NOT supported by the details in the passage?

A   The FBI's Ten Most Wanted Fugitives list has changed with the times.
B   "Most Wanted" style lists existed before the FBI began their list.
C   The majority of the fugitives that have appeared on the FBI's Ten Most Wanted Fugitives list have been apprehended.
D   The FBI began their list in response to the rise of crime in Chicago in the 1930s.

30. What is the tone of the passage?

A   informational
B   persuasive
C   argumentative
D   nostalgic

31. According to the passage, where did the idea for the FBI's Most Wanted Fugitives list come from?

   A   the 1930 "Public Enemies" List
   B   J. Edgar Hoover
   C   an International News Service reporter
   D   Joe Aiello

32. According to the passage, how has the list changed since its start in 1950?

   A   The list features more international fugitives.
   B   The list features more bootleggers.
   C   The list will no longer feature bank robbers.
   D   The list is no longer effective.

33. Compare and contrast the 1930 Chicago Crime Commission's "Public Enemies" list with the FBI's Ten Most Wanted Fugitives list. Use details from the story to support your answer.

   _____

   _____

   _____

   _____

   _____

   _____

   _____

   _____

   _____

   _____

   _____

   _____

Answer Sheet

1. (A) (B) (C) (D)
2. (A) (B) (C) (D)
3. (A) (B) (C) (D)
4. (A) (B) (C) (D)
5. (A) (B) (C) (D)
6. use space provided
7. (A) (B) (C) (D)
8. (A) (B) (C) (D)
9. (A) (B) (C) (D)
10. (A) (B) (C) (D)
11. use space provided
12. (A) (B) (C) (D)
13. (A) (B) (C) (D)
14. (A) (B) (C) (D)
15. (A) (B) (C) (D)
16. (A) (B) (C) (D)
17. use space provided

18. (A) (B) (C) (D)
19. (A) (B) (C) (D)
20. (A) (B) (C) (D)
21. (A) (B) (C) (D)
22. use space provided
23. (A) (B) (C) (D)
24. (A) (B) (C) (D)
25. (A) (B) (C) (D)
26. (A) (B) (C) (D)
27. use space provided
28. (A) (B) (C) (D)
29. (A) (B) (C) (D)
30. (A) (B) (C) (D)
31. (A) (B) (C) (D)
32. (A) (B) (C) (D)
33. use space provided

Answers to Chapters and Brain Boosters

Chapter 1

1. C
2. D
3. In order to get a top-score response for your open-response questions, remember the four keys listed below. Each key will unlock your chance to get full credit for an open response question.

   - Read the question carefully to make sure that you are clear on what it is asking.

   - Provide a response that is accurate, complete, and answers the question.

   - Supply details and information from the passage to strengthen your answer. Remember, to some extent open-response questions are your opportunity to persuade your reader. Go for it!

   - Keep your answer focused and never rely on your memory when providing supporting details. ALWAYS look back at the passage.

Example of a Top-Score Response

Six states and three countries probably rejected the garbage barge because of its bulk and its smell. Loaded with 3,186 tons of garbage, the garbage barge, whose actual name is the Mobro Barge, was not a very pleasant visitor. The fact that it sailed around in early summer heat most likely made it smell even worse!

Officials discovering that the trash was hazardous most likely had a lot to do their rejection of the garbage barge. Perhaps if officials hadn't discovered hospital waste, the barge would have been welcomed into one of the six states or three countries that rejected it.

Chapter 2

1. A
2. B
3. D
4. C
5. In order to get a top-score response for your open-response questions, remember the four keys listed below. Each key will unlock your chance to get full credit for an open-response question.

   - Read the question carefully to make sure that you are clear on what it is asking.

   - Provide a response that is accurate, complete, and answers the question.

   - Supply details and information from the passage to strengthen your answer. Remember, to some extent open-response questions are your opportunity to persuade your reader. Go for it!

   - Keep your answer focused and never rely on your memory when providing supporting details. ALWAYS look back at the passage.

Example of a Top-Score Response

The first point that scientists agree upon regarding the extinction of the dinosaurs is that Earth went through a permanent global climatic change 65 million years ago. If the climate changed, the dinosaurs may not have been suited for the new climate. This is a likely cause of the dinosaurs becoming extinct.

The second point that scientists agree on is that there were temporary environmental changes that may have been the result of a massive terrestrial, or earthly, disturbance. This disturbance threw soot and dust up into the air causing short-term acid rain, release of poisonous gases, and cooling. Acid rain and the release of poisonous gases most likely made it difficult for dinosaurs to breathe.

The third point that scientists agree upon is that many life forms—not just dinosaurs—both vertebrate and invertebrate marine and terrestrial organisms, went extinct, which means that even if dinosaurs survived the permanent global climatic change and temporary environmental changes, they would not have had much to feed on, and eventually, they would starve to death.

Chapter 3

1. A
2. D
3. D
4. A
5. In order to get a top-score response for your open-response questions, remember the four keys listed below. Each key will unlock your chance to get full credit for an open-response question.

   - Read the question carefully to make sure that you are clear on what it is asking.

   - Provide a response that is accurate, complete, and answers the question.

   - Supply details and information from the passage to strengthen your answer. Remember, to some extent open-response questions are your opportunity to persuade your reader. Go for it!

   - Keep your answer focused and never rely on your memory when providing supporting details. ALWAYS look back at the passage.

Example of a Top-Score Response

In the passage, the word <u>concentrated</u> *means intense or strong. The fact that you can achieve a sunburn faster using the device makes it clear that the device produces a light that is stronger, or more intense that regular sunlight.*

It is important for scientists to work with a device that speeds up the sunburn process, because scientists are trying to create products that will protect us from the Sun's harsh rays. The faster that scientists can experiment with the effects of sunlight on human skin, the faster that they can ensure that we don't damage our skin while out under sunny skies.

Chapter 4

1. C

2. In order to get a top-score response for your open-response questions, remember the four keys listed below. Each key will unlock your chance to get full credit for an open-response question.

    *   Read the question carefully to make sure that you are clear on what it is asking.

    *   Provide a response that is accurate, complete, and answers the question.

    *   Supply details and information from the passage to strengthen your answer. Remember, to some extent open-response questions are your opportunity to persuade your reader. Go for it!

    *   Keep your answer focused and never rely on your memory when providing supporting details. ALWAYS look back at the passage.

Example of a Top-Score Response

Some facts about birds from this passage are as follows:

*   *An albatross can sleep while flying. It can sleep while flying at twenty-five miles per hour.*

*   *Lovebirds are small parakeets who live in pairs. Male lovebirds have brighter colors than the females.*

3. B

4. C

5. In order to get a top-score response for your open-response questions, remember the four keys listed below. Each key will unlock your chance to get full credit for an open-response question.

    *   Read the question carefully to make sure that you are clear on what it is asking.

    *   Provide a response that is accurate, complete, and answers the question.

    *   Supply details and information from the passage to strengthen your answer. Remember, to some extent open-response questions are your opportunity to persuade your reader. Go for it!

    *   Keep your answer focused and never rely on your memory when providing supporting details. ALWAYS look back at the passage.

Example of a Top-Score Response

Some opinions that the author shares with the reader in this article are as follows:

- *If you were contemplating an acting career, perhaps you should consider checking out what Bollywood has to offer.*

- *You may want to brush up on your dance moves before you head to Bollywood because there are least five sing-a-long dance routines in each movie.*

- *You would most likely spend more time rehearsing movie scenes because the movies run two-and-a-half hours long.*

You may have found other opinions. For full credit you should include as many different opinion as you can find.

Brain Booster # 1

1. A
2. B
3. C
4. A list of opinions in this article is as follows:

   - *Whether you sleep in it, play sports in it, bum around the house in it, or wear it with your favorite jeans, chances are there's a story behind your favorite T-shirt.*

   - *Nowadays, most of us consider T-shirts a staple in our wardrobes.*

   - *Comfortable, casual, and always in style, T-shirts are tops above the rest.*

5. In order to get a top-score response for your open-response questions, remember the four keys listed below. Each key will unlock your chance to get full credit for an open-response question.

   - Read the question carefully to make sure that you are clear on what it is asking.

   - Provide a response that is accurate, complete, and answers the question.

   - Supply details and information from the passage to strengthen your answer. Remember, to some extent open-response questions are your opportunity to persuade your reader. Go for it!

   - Keep your answer focused and never rely on your memory when providing supporting details. ALWAYS look back at the passage.

Example of a Top-Score Response

I think that the invention of the T-shirt was important because T-shirts are not only comfortable, but they are great to wear in warmer weather. In addition, you can tell a lot about a person based on the type of T-shirt they wear. T-shirts were definitely an important invention for soldiers. Without T-shirts to keep them cool, you can imagine that the soldiers would have been pretty uncomfortable.

Chapter 5

1. C

2. A

3. In order to get a top-score response for your open-response questions, remember the four keys listed below. Each key will unlock your chance to get full credit for an open-response question.

- Read the question carefully to make sure that you are clear on what it is asking.

- Provide a response that is accurate, complete, and answers the question.

- Supply details and information from the passage to strengthen your answer. Remember, to some extent open-response questions are your opportunity to persuade your reader. Go for it!

- Keep your answer focused and never rely on your memory when providing supporting details. ALWAYS look back at the passage.

Example of a Top-Score Response

The theme of this passage is that the birth of a sport in America that has a long history in another country, often takes time to catch on. Up until 1992, sumo wrestling did not exist in the United States, with the exception of Hawaii. Now, though, the sport is beginning to gain some popularity, and some wrestlers are hopeful that the sport will be included in future Olympic games.

4. In order to get a top-score response for your open-response questions, remember the four keys listed above.

Example of a Top-Score Response

The main idea of this passage is not to give up no matter what opposition you face, and to follow your dreams. That's what William Hanna and Joseph Barbera, two young MGM animators, did when they created a cartoon of their own for MGM. Not only did Tom and Jerry receive a warm welcome, it went on to win seven Academy Awards!

For seventeen years, Hanna and Barbara made more then 120 of the cat and mouse cartoons. When MGM decided to drop the Tom and Jerry cartoon due to financial constraints, Hanna and Barbera didn't give up their dreams. They went on to create their own animation studio and created more made-for-television cartoons.

5. A
6. A
7. D

Chapter 6

1. A
2. C
3. A
4. D
5. In order to get a top-score response for your open-response questions, remember the four keys listed below. Each key will unlock your chance to get full credit for an open-response question.

   - Read the question carefully to make sure that you are clear on what it is asking.

   - Provide a response that is accurate, complete, and answers the question.

   - Supply details and information from the passage to strengthen your answer. Remember, to some extent open-response questions are your opportunity to persuade your reader. Go for it!

   - Keep your answer focused and never rely on your memory when providing supporting details. ALWAYS look back at the passage.

Example of a Top-Score Response

Zena most likely knew that dirty people do not necessarily the only ones who get acne. Before Zena became a skin doctor, or dermatologist, she had to go to medical school to learn about skin disorders, including acne. While Zena tells the high school students that stress and elevated levels of testosterone can lead to acne, Zena is firm when she informs the audience that dirty people are not the only ones to get acne. Zena states, "Bacteria lurk in everyone's skin, whether you're clean or dirty, fourteen or forty-five."

6. A

Chapter 7

1. C
2. C
3. B
4. In order to get a top-score response for your open-response questions, remember the four keys listed below. Each key will unlock your chance to get full credit for an open-response question.

   - Read the question carefully to make sure that you are clear on what it is asking.

   - Provide a response that is accurate, complete, and answers the question.

   - Supply details and information from the passage to strengthen your answer. Remember, to some extent open-response questions are your opportunity to persuade your reader. Go for it!

   - Keep your answer focused and never rely on your memory when providing supporting details. ALWAYS look back at the passage.

Example of a Top-Score Response

The words that the author chose and the style that the author used to write this passage support the author's purpose in a variety of ways. Because the passage is about roller coasters, particularly the Cyclone, the author's style of writing fills you with a sense of movement and excitement. Reading the passage, you almost feel as if you are climbing up and up and ready to take the ride down. "Wheeee!!!" sets you up to fly freely with the author alongside you. In addition, the imagery, such as "the chink-chink-chink as the train pulls our car and the wood creaks a little just before we drop down" really makes you feel as if you are alongside the author on the famous roller coaster.

5. A
6. D

Brain Booster # 2

1. A
2. B
3. In order to get a top-score response for your open-response questions, remember the four keys listed below. Each key will unlock your chance to get full credit for an open-response question.

   - Read the question carefully to make sure that you are clear on what it is asking.

   - Provide a response that is accurate, complete, and answers the question.

   - Supply details and information from the passage to strengthen your answer. Remember, to some extent open-response questions are your opportunity to persuade your reader. Go for it!

   - Keep your answer focused and never rely on your memory when providing supporting details. ALWAYS look back at the passage.

Example of a Top-Score Response

The theme of the passage is that people love to be adventurous, often ignoring the risks involved. For example, each year people travel to Pamplona to run with the bulls. While the event is one that certainly gets the runners' adrenaline going, there have been more than two dozen deaths and hundreds of people injured by the bulls.

Chapter 8

1. A
2. C
3. A
4. B
5. In order to get a top-score response for your open-response questions, remember the four keys listed below. Each key will unlock your chance to get full credit for an open-response question.

   - Read the question carefully to make sure that you are clear on what it is asking.

   - Provide a response that is accurate, complete, and answers the question.

   - Supply details and information from the passage to strengthen your answer. Remember, to some extent open-response questions are your opportunity to persuade your reader. Go for it!

   - Keep your answer focused and never rely on your memory when providing supporting details. ALWAYS look back at the passage.

Example of a Top-Score Response

Ellen MacArthur is clearly more courageous than Roxy. Ellen is determined and passionate about sailing. She has been on dangerous trips and holds many sailing records despite the early setbacks in her career. Roxy, on the other hand, talks about riding coasters, but lacks the courage to do so.

Chapter 9

1. B
2. A
3. B
4. A
5. In order to get a top-score response for your open-response questions, remember the four keys listed below. Each key will unlock your chance to get full credit for an open-response question.

   - Read the question carefully to make sure that you are clear on what it is asking.

   - Provide a response that is accurate, complete, and answers the question.

   - Supply details and information from the passage to strengthen your answer. Remember, to some extent open-response questions are your opportunity to persuade your reader. Go for it!

   - Keep your answer focused and never rely on your memory when providing supporting details. ALWAYS look back at the passage.

Example of a Top-Score Response

Poe claims his poem is immortal because of the name he has hidden inside the lines of the poem. He states this in his last two lines: "Stable, opaque, immortal—all by dint/Of the dear names that lie concealed within't." He means this in two ways. He is flattering Sarah Anna Lewis by telling her she'll live forever in the poem. He also means that future generations will read the poem because they'll want to figure out the puzzle.

6. C

Chapter 10

1. B
2. D
3. A
4. C

Brain Booster # 3

1. C
2. A
3. D
4. A
5. B

Chapter 11

1. D
2. A
4. B
3. B

Chapter 12

1. A
2. C
3. B
4. A
5. B

Chapter 13

1. D
2. A
3. A
4. D
5. List events as the happen in the story. Make sure you focus on the proper sequence of events.

Example of a Top-Score Response

The sequence of events in the passage is as follows:

- *Olivia decides to study eyebrows.*

- *Olivia observes her family members' eyebrows, but because she knows their expressions so well, studying their eyebrows bores her.*

- *She shifts her attention to her neighbor, Mrs. Huber. She positions herself outside Mrs. Huber's kitchen window and is caught snooping by Mrs. Huber.*

- *Olivia tells Mrs. Huber about her eyebrow project. Mrs. Huber tells Olivia that as a result of surgery she had years ago, that part of her face is numb. Olivia asks to interview Mrs. Huber.*

Brain Booster # 4

1. B
2. A
3. In order to get a top-score response for your open-response questions, remember the four keys listed below. Each key will unlock your chance to get full credit for an open-response question.

- Read the question carefully to make sure that you are clear on what it is asking.

- Provide a response that is accurate, complete, and answers the question.

- Supply details and information from the passage to strengthen your answer. Remember, to some extent open-response questions are your opportunity to persuade your reader. Go for it!

- Keep your answer focused and never rely on your memory when providing supporting details. ALWAYS look back at the passage.

Example of a Top-Score Response

Based on the fact that Jupiter had fireballs in its atmosphere because of fragments of the Shoemaker-Levy 9's bombarding it, you can conclude that the comet was an extremely powerful one. The comet's great size supports this conclusion as well.

4. A
5. C

Chapter 14

1. D
2. A
3. C
4. B
5. B

Chapter 15

1. A
2. B
3. A
4. D
5. In order to get a top-score response for your open-response questions, remember the four keys listed below. Each key will unlock your chance to get full credit for an open-response question.

   - Read the question carefully to make sure that you are clear on what it is asking.

   - Provide a response that is accurate, complete, and answers the question.

   - Supply details and information from the passage to strengthen your answer. Remember, to some extent open-response questions are your opportunity to persuade your reader. Go for it!

   - Keep your answer focused and never rely on your memory when providing supporting details. ALWAYS look back at the passage.

Example of a Top-Score Response

This graphic organizer collects together information on the ways the goliath bird-eating spider hunts and the ways in which it can protect itself. It defines what the spider is and then gives us dietary information, hunting information, and information on the defensive hairs the spider can use for protection.

6. In order to get a top-score response for your open-response questions, remember the four keys listed above.

Example of a Top Scoring Response

The passage mentions that the goliath bird-eating spider also eats the occasional bat and hatchling bird. This information should be included to complete the circle in the web.

Chapter 16

1. B
2. B
3. C
4. A

Brain Booster # 5

1. B
2. D
3. B
4. A

Answers and Explanations for the Practice Test

1. **A** This question is asking you to find the best meaning for the word *materialized* as it appears in the passage. Read each answer choice and consider what you know about using context clues.

    (A) *Materialized* may mean showed up. Look back at the sentence. It's possible that showed up is a good fit for the word materialized in this sentence. A rescue party never showed up. Read the following answer choices before choosing an answer.

    (B) *Disappeared* doesn't make much sense in the context of the sentence. A rescue party never disappeared. That doesn't mean anything in regard to the story.

    (C) *Lost them* doesn't make much sense in the context of the sentence. A rescue party never lost them. In the story, a rescue party never found them.

    (D) *Sailed away* doesn't make much sense in the context of the sentence. A rescue party never sailed away. In the story, a rescue party never sailed to them.

2. **C** This question is asking you about a cause and an effect. Read each answer choice and consider what you know about cause and effect.

    (A) It's unlikely that Shackelton led the expedition because he took pleasure in sailing in bad weather. That doesn't make sense in light of the passage.

    (B) It's unlikely that Shackelton led the expedition because he wanted to be the captain of *The Endurance*. There is no reference to this in the passage.

    (C) Based upon the passage, it is true that Shackelton led the expedition because he wanted to cross the Antarctic continent. You are told that in paragraph 1.

    (D) It's unlikely that Shackelton led the expedition because he wanted to go on a long journey. There is no reference to this in the passage.

3. **C** This question is asking you in what genre this passage is written. Read each answer choice and consider what you know about genre.

    (A) Is this passage an example of satire? Satire is a critical and pointed form of humor. This passage isn't poking fun of anything, so it is not satire.

    (B) Is this passage an example of drama? There is no dialogue, no stage direction, or anything else that would lead us to believe this was intended to be performed on stage. It is not drama.

    (C) Is this passage an example of biography? It seems to be. It is about the life of Ernest Schackelton. Read the following answer choices before choosing an answer.

    (D) Is this passage a newspaper article? It's unlikely because it spans a wide range of time, instead of focusing on current and immediate events.

4. **C** This question is asking you to find the main idea of the passage. Read each answer choice and consider what you know about genre.

(A) Is the main purpose of the passage to prove that *The Endurance* really existed and set forth in 1958? This date conflicts with dates mentioned in the passage. This answer cannot be correct.

(B) Is the main purpose of the passage to provide details about the ship that Shackleton sailed? The passage is more concerned about the story behind the ship's inhabitants rather than details about the ship itself.

(C) Is the main purpose of the passage to share the amazing story of Shackleton and his crew's survival? This seems to best fit with the content and tone of the passage.

(D) Is the main purpose to scare people into never trying to cross the Antarctic continent? There is no reference in the passage to keeping people from trying for themselves.

5. **D** This question asks you about tone. Read each answer choice and consider what you know about tone.

(A) Is the tone of this passage pessimistic? While the crew endured numerous hardships, the tone is not pessimistic.

(B) Is the tone at the end of this passage humorous? No, that is not the appropriate way to describe the tone at the end of the passage.

(C) Is the tone at the end of the passage ironic? No, that does not seem relevant to this passage.

(D) Is the tone at the end of the passage reverential? Yes, that does seem to fit. *Reverential* means respectful. There is a sense of respect for Ernest Schackelton and his crew at the conclusion of this passage.

6. In order to get a top-score response for your open-response questions, remember the four keys listed below. Each key will unlock your chance to get full credit for an open-response question.

- Read the question carefully to make sure that you are clear on what it is asking.

- Provide a response that is accurate, complete, and answers the question.

- Supply details and information from the passage to strengthen your answer. Remember, to some extent open-response questions are your opportunity to persuade your reader. Go for it!

- Keep your answer focused and never rely on your memory when providing supporting details. ALWAYS look back at the passage.

Example of Top-Score Response

If I were writing an article arguing that Ernest Shackleton was a brave man, I would tell about his expedition on The Endurance. Shackleton started out on the voyage with a goal of crossing the Antarctic continent; little did he know that The Endurance would put him to many tests.

The Endurance suffered its first mishap when it was trapped in an ice pack. Shackleton and his men did not panic; rather, they planned for a long-term survival aboard the ship. For a year, all seemed fine until The Endurance began to sink. Shackelton and the entire crew escaped on a drifting ice flow and waited to be rescued in vain.

Shackleton later led his men to Elephant Island. Knowing that it would only be a matter of time before the men died of either starvation or hypothermia, Ernest Shackleton then made the bravest decision of his life—he picked his five bravest men, and together they set sail and eventually reached South Georgia Island. Shackelton and his men had to cross mountains before they were able to organize a rescue for the men they left behind. The whole ordeal lasted almost two years before the men all returned home—not a single life was lost. Shackelton's bravery and leadership was evident.

7. **B**   This question asks you to make an inference. Read each answer choice and consider what you know about inferences.
    (A) Is *The Big Book of World Records* the least likely place you would find information on the Thrust SSC? Because the SSC broke the land speed record and is the first car to break to sound barrier, you might find information on the Thrust SSC in *The Big Book of World Records.*
    (B) Is *Family Car Buyer's Digest* a magazine that you would find an article on the Thrust SSC? Chances are that you would not find an article about the Thrust SSC in this magazine. The Thrust SSC is not the kind of cars just anybody could buy and it would most likely not be described as a "family car." This is the correct answer.
    (C) Would you find information in *the Science section of a newspaper*? Given the high-tech nature of the SSC, you might find an article on the Thrust SSC in in the "Science" section of a newspaper.
    (D) Is *an encyclopedia* a good place to find information on the SSC? While it may not provide you with as much information as answer choices (C) and (A), it is still more likely that you would find information on the SSC in an encyclopedia than you would in *Family Car Buyer's Digest.* This answer is not the best choice.

8. **C** This question asks you to summarize the passage.

(A) Does the narrator really intend *to be the next driver of the SSC*? The passage makes it clear that, while she would like to drive the SSC, the narrator knows this is unlikely to ever happen.

(B) While the *use of jet engines* is mentioned in the passage, it is not the main point of the passage. This is too specific to be a summary of the entire passage.

(C) This passage does focus on *the many elements that make the SSC the fastest car ever created*. Furthermore, the narrator is personally impressed with the speed of the SSC. This is the best answer choice.

(D) The answer choice does agree with the information in the passage, but it is not a proper summary. This detail is too specific to be considered a summary of the entire passage.

9. **A** This question asks you to use inference to figure out what the sentence means.

(A) Does the sentence mean that *the Thrust SSC travels at a speed much faster than what you are used to travelling*? It states that "you will have to buckle in tight for a ride in the Thrust SSC or risk getting whiplash" which most likely means that the Thrust SSC travels at a much faster speed than usual.

(B) Does the sentence mean *be careful: Thrust SSC does not offer a smooth ride to its riders*? The passage doesn't mention anything about the Thrust SSC not offering a smooth ride.

(C) Does the sentence mean *a ride in the Thrust SSC often causes people to have stiff necks*? There is no mention of stiff necks in the passage.

(D) Does the sentence mean that *if you drive the Thrust SSC, you need to be sure that you wear a neck brace*? No. There is no mention of a neck brace in the passage.

10. **D** This question asks you to make an inference. Read all the answer choices and consider what you know about inferences.
(A) Does the fact that the SSC uses a parachute braking system have anything to do with the narrator hitting the gas and getting to school faster? It does not.
(B) Does the fact that the Thrust SSC is on display at a museum in the United Kingdom have anything to do with the narrator getting to school faster? While it's interesting information, it does not have to do with the narrator getting to school faster.
(C) Does the fact that Thrust SSC weighs one ton have anything to do with the narrator getting to school faster? It does not.
(D) Does the fact that the Thrust SSC accelerates quickly have anything to do with the narrator getting to school faster? It does. If the car accelerates faster, then when the narrator hits the gas, she will most likely get to school faster.

11. In order to get a top-score response for your open-response questions, remember the four keys listed below. Each key will unlock your chance to get full credit for an open-response question.

- Read the question carefully to make sure that you are clear on what it is asking.

- Provide a response that is accurate, complete, and answers the question.

- Supply details and information from the passage to strengthen your answer. Remember, to some extent open-response questions are your opportunity to persuade your reader. Go for it!

- Keep your answer focused and never rely on your memory when providing supporting details. ALWAYS look back at the passage.

Example of Top-Score Response

The narrator's tone in the passage is enthusiastic and passionate about the Thrust SSC. The narrator wishes that she could go faster, and the Thrust SSC appears as her answer to doing just that. It is the narrator's dream to drive the world's fastest land vehicle. The author also states that she is sad that the SSC is now in a museum and will most likely not be making another run.

Furthermore, the author shows her reverence to the Thrust SSC by knowing all there is to know about it. She has clearly done a lot of reading and investigation when it comes to the Thrust SSC's capabilities.

While the narrator knows that she will not likely have a chance to drive the Thrust SSC just yet, she ends on a playful, optimistic note. The narrator says she would gladly volunteer to drive the car if they ever take it on another run.

12. **B**   This question asks you to use context clues to determine the meaning of a word. Read all the answer choices and consider what you know about context clues.

(A) Does the word *controversy* mean *confused* in the sentence indicated? Look at the sentence. The word *confused* does not make sense according to the context clues.

(B) Does the word *controversy* mean *debate* in the sentence indicated? Look at the sentence. The word *debate* does make sense according to the context clues. This is the correct answer.

(C) Does the word *controversy* mean *uncertainty* in the sentence indicated? Look at the sentence. The word *uncertainty* does not make sense according to the context clues.

(D) Does the word *controversy* mean *beliefs* in the sentence indicated? Look at the sentence. The word *beliefs* do not make sense according to the context clues.

13. **B**   This question asks you to find the sequence of the passage. Read all the answer choices and consider what you know about sequence.

(A) This choice is not how the narrator's interest in da Vinci's Mona Lisa began, although the narrator did go on to read articles about da Vinci after her interest was piqued.

(B) This choice is stated in the first sentence of the passage. Before you choose this answer choice, read the remaining answer choices.

(C) While this choice may be true, it is not stated in the passage. We may assume this to be true because the teacher is teaching about the Mona Lisa, but all that we are told is that the narrator is studying it in art history class.

(D) This information does not appear in the passage that you read.

14. **C**   This question asks you to review and recall details from the passage. Read all the answer choices and consider what you know about details.

(A) While this answer choice is true, it does not have anything to do with whether or not da Vinci's painting was of Mona Lisa Gherardini.

(B) Again, while this answer choice is true, it does not have anything to do with whether or not da Vinci's painting was of Mona Lisa Gherardini.

(C) This answer choice does acknowledge the doubt surrounding da Vinci's paining being a portrait for Mona Lisa Gherardini. Look back at the passage to verify that this answer choice is in fact true.

(D) While this answer choice is true based on the passage, it does not have anything to do with whether or not da Vinci's painting was of Mona Lisa Gherardini.

Know It All! High School Reading

15. **A** This question asks you about tone. Read all the answer choices and consider what you know about tone.
(A) Is the narrator in the passage *curious*? The narrator goes to the library to do her own investigation on the subject of the "Mona Lisa." This suggests that the narrator wanted to know more. This is the correct answer.
(B) Is the narrator *bored*? No, she is not. Based on the passage, the narrator is interested in the topic.
(C) Is the narrator *excited*? She may be, but she seems to be more curious than excited about this topic.
(D) The narrator does not seem to be *annoyed* at all throughout the passage.

16. **B** This question asks you to find the main idea of the passage. Read all the answer choices and consider what you know about main idea.
(A) While da Vinci may have painted a lot of portraits of women, that is not what this passage is about. This passage discusses one portrait of *one* woman that he painted.
(B) This statement is true. The passage is mostly about the fact that we may never know the identity of the woman in the Mona Lisa. Before you choose this answer, read the following answer choices.
(C) This is not what the passage is about.
(D) While this detail is mentioned in the passage, it is by no means what the passage is about overall.

17. In order to get a top-score response for your open-response questions, remember the four keys listed below. Each key will unlock your chance to get full credit for an open-response question.

- Read the question carefully to make sure that you are clear on what it is asking.

- Provide a response that is accurate, complete, and answers the question.

- Supply details and information from the passage to strengthen your answer. Remember, to some extent open-response questions are your opportunity to persuade your reader. Go for it!

- Keep your answer focused and never rely on your memory when providing supporting details. ALWAYS look back at the passage.

Example of Top-Score Response

The debate that the narrator discusses in the passage has to do with the identity of the mystery woman in Leonardo da Vinci's Mona Lisa. The narrator becomes interested in who the portrait depicts in her art history class.

The narrator uncovers that there are a number of candidates who may be the real Mona Lisa. While the narrator details some of the possibilities: the painting may depict Mona Lisa Gherardini; it may depict a noblewoman that da Vinci knew; or it may be a feminized self-portrait. The narrator concludes that there is no answer to the controversy over the identity of the woman in da Vinci's portrait.

18. **D** This question asks you to find the meaning of a word based on context clues. Read all the answer choices and consider what you know about context clues.
    (A) Does *artifacts* mean *discarded things* based on the context? No, it does not.
    (B) Does *artifacts* mean *expensive things* based on the context? While artifacts may very well be worth a lot of money, in regard to the passage this answer choice is not correct.
    (C) Does *artifacts* mean *used goods* based on the context? While artifacts are most often used goods, in regard to the passage this answer choice is not correct.
    (D) Does *artifacts* mean *objects from the past* based on the context? Yes, it does. Considering that the passage, this answer choice is most applicable.

19. **B** This question asks you to recall the sequence of the passage. Read all the answer choices and consider what you know about sequence.
    (A) Did this event happen first? Reread the passage. The passage mentions a legal battle, but it occurs near the very end of the passage.
    (B) Did this event occur first? Reread back to the passage. Based on the passage, this event was the first step in hunting for the treasure. It occurred before all the events mentioned as answer choices. This is the correct choice.
    (C) Did this event occur first? Reread to the passage. Based on the passage, this event happened after the event in answer choice (B).
    (D) Did this event occur first? Reread to the passage. Based on the passage, this event happened after the event in answer choice (B).

20. **D**   This question asks you to describe the main characters of the passage.
(A) Were Thompson and Evans *pessimistic*? Given the slim chances of finding the treasure, it is unlikely that two pessimistic people would have looked for it.
(B) Were Thompson and Evans *greedy*? The passage suggests that they shared some of the valuable objects with museums and other public institutions. This does not fit the idea that they were greedy.
(C) Were Thompson and Evans easily *discouraged*? Look back at the passage. Despite setbacks, the two kept searching. This is the opposite of easily discouraged.
(D) Were Thompson and Evans *persistent*? Look back at the passage. Despite the slim odds and various setbacks, the two treasure hunters never quit the search. They were persistent. This is the best answer choice.

21. **B**   This question asks you to find the main idea of the passage. Read all the answer choices and consider what you know about main idea.
(A) Does this answer choice best describe what happens in the passage? The ship did sink, but this answer choice leaves out all the information about finding the treasure. This is not the correct answer.
(B) Does this answer choice best describe what happens in the passage? Yes. The passage is about the *SS Central America* being found and the treasures being recovered.
(C) Does this answer choice best describe what happens in the passage? No. This is only a detail mentioned in the passage.
(D) Does this answer choice best describe what happens in the passage? No. This is detail is not mentioned in the passage.

22. In order to get a top-score response for your open-response questions, remember the four keys listed below. Each key will unlock your chance to get full credit for an open-response question.

- Read the question carefully to make sure that you are clear on what it is asking.

- Provide a response that is accurate, complete, and answers the question.

- Supply details and information from the passage to strengthen your answer. Remember, to some extent open-response questions are your opportunity to persuade your reader. Go for it!

- Keep your answer focused and never rely on your memory when providing supporting details. ALWAYS look back at the passage.

Example of Top-Score Response

If I were to write my own article about the SS Central America, I would use a lot of the information from the passage, including information about Thompson and Evans' endeavors to recover the missing gold. I would also include information about Nemo, the undersea robot. I would note what the team discovered in 1987, such as the nineteenth-century artifacts, the wreck of the SS Central America, and the coins.

I would look for more information about this event in the history section of the library. Another place I may look for information would be in books about famous treasures recovered, or in books about ships that sunk with treasures.

23. **B** This question asks you to use context clues to find the meaning of a word. Read all the answer choices and consider what you know about context clues.
    (A) Does the word *ornamented* mean *interesting*? No, it does not.
    (B) Does the word *ornamented* mean *decorated*? Yes, it does. This is the correct answer choice.
    (C) Does the word *ornamented* mean *unattractive*? No, it does not.
    (D) Does the word *ornamented* mean *enthusiastic*? No, it does not.

24. **B** This question asks you to recall a detail. Read all the answer choices and consider what you know about details.
    (A) Does Mardi Gras take place the *night before the parade begins*? Look back at the passage. No, it does not. The parades are a part of Mardi Gras celebrations.
    (B) Does Mardi Gras take place *the night before Lent begins*? Look back at the passage. Yes, it does take place the night before Lent begins. Before you choose this answer, read the remaining answer choices.
    (C) Does Mardi Gras take place the *night before Easter begins*? Look back at the passage. No, it does not.
    (D) Does Mardi Gras take place *the night before New Year's Day*? Look back at the passage. No, it does not. New Year's Day is not mentioned at all in the passage.

25. **A** This question asks you to recall a detail. Read all the answer choices and consider what you know about details.
    (A) Do people collect *throws* during Mardi Gras? Look back at the passage. According to the passage, they do. This is the correct answer.
    (B) Do people collect *coupons* during Mardi Gras? Look back at the passage. It does not mention people collecting coupons.
    (C) Do people collect *masks* during Mardi Gras? Look back at the passage. It mentions the masked balls that were once part of Mardi Gras, but it does not mention people collecting masks.
    (D) Do people collect *krewes* during Mardi Gras? Look back at the passage. Krewes are what you call the groups that help organize Mardi Gras. People are in krewes, but they don't collect them.

Know It All! High School Reading

26. **A**   This question asks you to summarize the passage. Read all the answer choices and consider what you know about summarizing.
(A) Does this statement summarize what the passage is about? The passage focuses on the history and traditions of Mardi Gras. This is the best answer choice.
(B) Is this what the passage is about? While krewes are mentioned in the passage, it is not what the majority of the passage is about.
(C) Is this what the passage is about? While the rules against dancing in the streets are mentioned in the passage, it is not what the majority of the passage is about.
(D) This choice is incorrect because it misrepresents a detail from the passage. People used to celebrate Mardi Gras by holding masked balls in their homes. This answer choice is incorrect.

27. In order to get a top-score response for your open-response questions, remember the four keys listed below. Each key will unlock your chance to get full credit for an open-response question.

- Read the question carefully to make sure that you are clear on what it is asking.

- Provide a response that is accurate, complete, and answers the question.

- Supply details and information from the passage to strengthen your answer. Remember, to some extent open-response questions are your opportunity to persuade your reader. Go for it!

- Keep your answer focused and never rely on your memory when providing supporting details. ALWAYS look back at the passage.

Example of Top-Score Response

The tone of this passage is fun and informative. The narrator provides details about the history of Mardi Gras celebration, as well as interesting facts. The narrator explains the history of the celebration which dates back to the seventeenth century. The narrator explains the religious origins of the celebration and goes into detail explaining the origins of the krewes.

The narrator keeps the tone playful by stating that Mardi Gras is a time to have fun. The narrator uses informal language, like the word "shenanigans." The narrator also gives readers the best spot to watch the Mardi Gras parades.

28. **D** This question asks you to use context clues to find the meaning of a word. Read all the answer choices and consider what you know about context clues.

(A) Does the word *anonymity* mean *honesty*? There is nothing in context to suggest that a fugitive would be honest. This answer choice is incorrect.

(B) Does the word *anonymity* mean *incompetence*? No, it does not. *Incompetence* means lack of ability. That does not make sense in this context.

(C) Does the word *anonymity* mean *confusion*? No, it does not. While a fugitive may be helped by confusion, this is not the best answer.

(D) Does the word *anonymity* mean *secrecy*? Yes, it does. Fugitives must keep their identities secret and the Most Wanted list makes it harder for them to do this. This is the correct answer.

29. **D** This question asks you to recall details from the passage. Read all the answer choices and consider what you know about details. Remember that you are looking for the answer that NOT supported by the details of the passage.

(A) Is it true that the FBI list has changed with the times? Yes it has, so this is not the correct answer choice.

(B) Did the Most Wanted style lists exist before the FBI began their list? Yes. The "public enemies" list is an example of an earlier list. This is not the correct answer choice.

(C) Have the majority of fugitives on the FBI's Ten Most Wanted Fugitives list been apprehended? According to the passage, yes they have. This is not the correct answer choice.

(D) Did the FBI start their list in response to the rise of crime in Chicago in the 1930s? No, this statement conflicts with the details in the passage. This is the correct answer choice.

30. **A** This question asks you about tone. Read all the answer choices and consider what you know about tone.

(A) Is the tone of the passage *informational*? You learn about the history of the FBI's Ten Most Wanted list. The passage's tone is informational. This is the correct answer.

(B) Is the tone of this passage *persuasive*? It doesn't try to persuade you to do anything. Therefore, it is not persuasive.

(C) Is the tone of this passage *argumentative*? No, it is not.

(D) Is the tone of this passage *nostalgic*? No, it is not.

31. **C** This question asks you to recall a detail from the passage. Read all the answer choices and consider what you know about details.
(A) Did the FBI get the idea for the Ten Most Wanted Fugitives list from the "public enemies" list of the Chicago Crime Commission? According to the passage, they did not. This is not the correct answer choice.
(B) Did J. Edgar Hoover come up with the idea? No, not according to the passage.
(C) Did the idea come from an International Services news reporter? According to the passage, the idea came from a story by an International Services news reporter of the toughest fugitives the FBI was searching for. This is the best answer choice.
(D) Did Joe Aiello come up with the idea? According to the passage, he was the head of the Moran Gang. He did not come up with the idea.

32. **A** This question asks you to recall a detail from the passage. Read all the answer choices and consider what you know about details.
(A) Does the passage say that *the list features more international fugitives*? It says this in the last paragraph. This is the correct answer.
(B) Does the passage claim that *the list features more bootleggers*? No, it does not. This answer choice is incorrect.
(C) Does the passage say *the list will no longer feature bank robbers*? The passage suggests that the kind of fugitive that appears on the list has changed, but it never states that a bank robber would never be put on the list again. This answer choice is incorrect.
(D) Does the passage state *the list is no longer effective*? Actually, the passage states just the opposite. This answer choice is incorrect.

33. In order to get a top-score response for your open-response questions, remember the four keys listed below. Each key will unlock your chance to get full credit for an open-response question.

- Read the question carefully to make sure that you are clear on what it is asking.

- Provide a response that is accurate, complete, and answers the question.

- Supply details and information from the passage to strengthen your answer. Remember, to some extent open-response questions are your opportunity to persuade your reader. Go for it!

- Keep your answer focused and never rely on your memory when providing supporting details. ALWAYS look back at the passage.

Example of Top-Score Response

Both the FBI's Ten Most Wanted Fugitives list and the Chicago Crime Commission's "public enemies" list featured suspected criminals considered dangerous to the public. Both lists have the same goal. The FBI and the Crime Commission wanted to shut criminals down by exposing them to the public.

Although they are similar in many ways, the Chicago Crime Commission's list existed nearly twenty years before the FBI list was started. The Crime Commission's list contained twenty-eight names, while the FBI list contains just ten names. Furthermore, the Crime Commission's list was a local list, created in response to an increase in crime in Chicago. The FBI list is an updated, international list that contains names submitted from national and foreign FBI branch offices.

Furthermore, the Chicago list featured gangsters while the FBI list features a broad variety of fugitives. The current Ten Most Wanted Fugitives list features foreign terrorists and members of South American drug cartels as well American fugitives.

If students need to know it,
it's in our Know It All! Guides!